SCHOLASTIC

National Curriculum
ENGLISH
Revision Guide

- ✓ Recap
- ✓ Revise
- ✓ Skills check

Ages 10–11
Year 6

KS2

SCHOLASTIC

National Curriculum
ENGLISH
Revision Guide

Book End, Range Road, Witney, Oxfordshire, OX29 0YD
Registered office: Westfield Road, Southam, Warwickshire CV47 0RA
www.scholastic.co.uk

© 2016, Scholastic Ltd

2 3 4 5 6 7 8 9   6 7 8 9 0 1 2 3 4 5

British Library Cataloguing-in-Publication Data
A catalogue record for this book is available from the British Library.

ISBN 978-1407-15974-4
Printed by Bell & Bain Ltd, Glasgow

Author
Lesley and Graham Fletcher

Editorial
Rachel Morgan, Tracey Cowell, Rebecca Rothwell, Jane Jackson and Sally Rigg

Series Design
Scholastic Design Team: Nicolle Thomas and Neil Salt

Design
Oxford Designers & Illustrators

Cover Design
Scholastic Design Team: Nicolle Thomas and Neil Salt

Cover Illustration
Shutterstock / © VIGE.CO

Illustration
Judy Brown

Contents

3

Vocabulary

Spelling

Reading

Using the revision guide

From 2016 new-style National Curriculum Tests will be introduced for children at the end of Key Stage 1 (7 years old) and at the end of Key Stage 2 (11 years old). Children will take tests in Grammar, Punctuation and Spelling, and Reading.

• These books are written by teachers for the National Curriculum to help children revise for end-of-year school tests in Grammar, Punctuation and Spelling, and Reading.

• Each book is split into five sections, which match the content to be covered by the tests.

• Revising for the tests will help children feel prepared and prevent them from worrying about the unknown.

• Use the books to practise skills 'little and often'. Don't attempt to do too much in one session.

• At the back of the book is a **Revision planner** to enable you to record what content has been covered and to prioritise what still needs to be done.

• A series of **Practice Tests** is available to help children towards the next stage of their preparations for National and school tests.

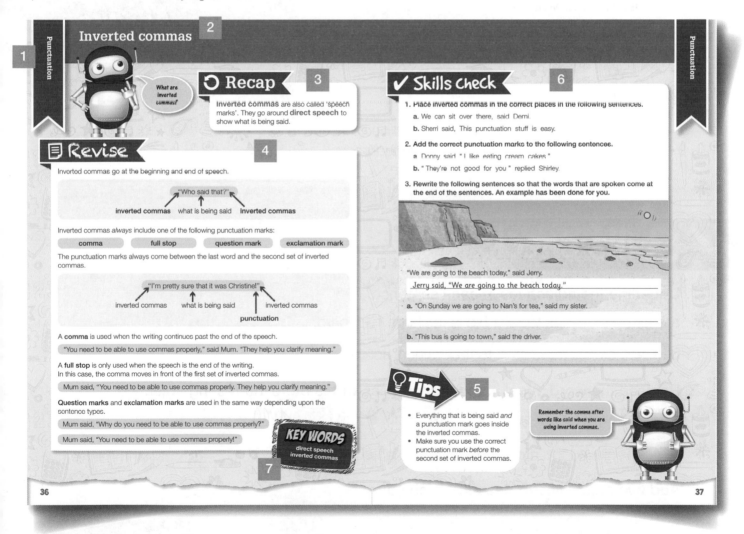

1 Chapter title

2 Topic title

3 Each page starts with a **recap** and a 'What is...' question which gives children a clear definition for the terminology used.

4 In the **revise** section there are clear teaching examples, using fun characters and clear illustrations and diagrams.

5 **Tips** are included to help show important points to remember and to give helpful strategies for remembering.

6 The **skills check** sections enable children to practise what they have learned using National Test-style questions.

7 **Key words** that children need to know are displayed. Definitions for these words can be found in the **Glossary**.

Adjectives

↻ Recap

What is an adjective?

An **adjective** describes a characteristic of a noun.

What a **beautiful** day!

The word **beautiful** is an adjective.

📄 Revise

Adjectives describe or modify nouns. They give us more detail and precision in our writing.

an **arduous** journey   a **wonderful** journey

↑   ↑

Not all adjectives describe characteristics we can see.
These adjectives describe very different journeys!

KEY WORDS
adjectives

✔ Skills check

1. **Underline the adjectives in each sentence.**

   a. The mischievous toddler hid in the large cupboard.

   b. It was a disastrous start to their annual holiday.

2. **Replace the word 'nice' in these sentences with a more interesting adjective.**

   a. Josh wrote a **nice** story.   Josh wrote a __outstanding__ story.

   b. Aliah enjoyed the **nice** pantomime.   Aliah enjoyed the __great__ pantomime.

3. **Add two adjectives to describe each noun.**

   a. __tall__,
   __rocky__ mountain

   b. __Brown__,
   __strong__ bear

Nouns and noun phrases

↻ Recap

A **noun** is a word for a person, place or thing. There are different types of noun: common and proper.

A **noun phrase** contains a noun as its main word and often contains a preposition or adjective: **next to the imposing school**.

What is a noun?

What is a noun phrase?

▤ Revise

Common nouns

Names of things			
vehicle	people	month	business
Names of emotions and qualities			
happiness	joy	bravery	comfort

Proper nouns

Names of places, people, days and months			
Vietnam	Mr Jones	February	Wednesday

All proper nouns must start with a capital letter.

A **noun phrase** can be made by putting adjectives and nouns together:

> long, hot month

Noun phrases may contain a noun and other words such as adjectives, determiners or prepositional phrases:

> in the forest   at the park   many children

These are all noun phrases.

Adjectives + nouns = noun phrase
the amazing magical machine
Remember: a phrase does not contain a verb!

✔ Skills Check

1. Last <u>summer</u> we went on holiday to <u>Turkey</u>. Our <u>pleasure</u> was only curtailed when it was time to come home!

   Tick the correct column to show the type of noun for each of the underlined words.

Word	Common noun	Proper noun
summer	✓	
Turkey		✓
pleasure	✓	

KEY WORDS

nouns
noun phrases

Verbs: present and past tense

↻ Recap

A **verb** tells you what is happening in a sentence. It is a doing word or being word.

The **tense** of a verb tells us when it happens: in the **present**, the **past** or the **future**.

What is a verb?

What is a tense?

KEY WORDS
verbs
tense (past, present)
progressive
future time

📄 Revise

Action verbs → I look   I wept

Simple present tense	Simple past tense
I look	I looked
he weeps	he wept
we drive	we drove

Use simple present or past for an action happening now (present) or an action that has already happened (past).

Being verbs → I am   I have

Present progressive tense	Past progressive tense
we **are** revising	we **were** revising

Use a **helper verb** (**to be** or **to have**) to show the action is/was continuous.

Helper verbs: to be or to have. Not all past tenses end in ed!

✔ Skills Check

1. **Complete the table using the correct form of the verbs.**

Present tense	Past tense	Present progressive	Past progressive
she brings	she brought	~~were~~ ~~revising~~ brings revising	~~was bringing~~
they catch ~~they are going to catch~~	they caught	they are going catch	they were catching
it grows	it grew	it is growing	it was growing
We	we built	We are building	we were building

2. **Complete the sentence using the past progressive form of the verb 'to work'.**

They _____ hard when the fire alarm stopped them.

Verbs: present perfect and past perfect tense

↻ Recap

The **present perfect** is used for an action which happened at some time in the past.

> I **have been** to the theme park before.

The **past perfect** is used for something which happened before another action in the past.

> Jack **had never been** to a live football game, before Saturday.

What is the present perfect?

What is the past perfect?

Tips

Perfect is a type of past tense. Don't be caught out by present perfect. It's still a past tense!

☰ Revise

Present perfect:
has/have + past tense of verb

They **have created** a beautiful picture.
↑ ↑
have + past tense of **create**
They **created** the picture.

She **has learnt** a new song.
↑ ↑
has + past tense of **learn**
She **learnt** a song in the past.

Past perfect:
had + past tense of verb

We **had enjoyed** the meal, until **the bill arrived**!
↑ ↑
action 1   action 2

I **had seen** the dark clouds before **the rain came**.
↑ ↑
action 1   action 2

KEY WORDS

present perfect
past perfect

✔ Skills Check

1. **Complete the sentences using the present perfect of each verb in bold.**

    a. go He __had went__ out to play.

    b. develop They __had__ _____ a method for baking perfect bread.

2. **Rewrite this sentence using the past perfect for the verb in bold.**

    I **enjoy** the film until the end spoilt it.

    __I had enjoyed until the end spoilt it.__

Verbs: tense consistency and Standard English

↻ Recap

What is tense consistency?

Tense consistency means having the same tense within a sentence.

Standard English is when the verb ending agrees with the thing or person doing the action. Standard English does not use slang or dialect words.

What is Standard English?

☰ Revise

Tense consistency: Use only one tense in a sentence:

They **booked** into their accommodation and **went** into the restaurant.

↖ both verbs in past tense ↗

Make the verb ending agree with the number of doers!

Standard English

A **singular** subject (or person doing it) must have a singular form of the verb:

Omar **visits** his grandparents. ⟶ Omar **was visiting** his grandparents.

one person = singular form of verb

A **plural** subject (or things doing it) must have a plural form of the verb:

The children **clean** their teeth. ⟶ The children **were cleaning** their teeth.

many people = plural form of verb

For collective nouns, one unit of people = singular form of the verb.

The team **is playing** in a local league.

KEY WORDS

singular
plural

✔ Skills check

1. Rewrite this sentence in Standard English: I sees a bird in the garden.

   I see' a bird on the garden

2. Choose the correct form of the verb to complete the sentence below.

   Amy _____ Jack to the concert. **Tick one.**

   is accompany ☐   have accompanied ☐   has accompanied ☑   has accompanies ☐

Modal verbs

What is a modal verb?

↻ Recap

Modal verbs are auxiliary verbs that change the meaning of other verbs. The modal verbs are:

| may | could | ought (to) | shall | will |

| might | should | would | can | must |

Least likely ←————————————→ Most likely

Modal verbs tell us how likely it is that something will happen.

Today is Monday so tomorrow **will** be Tuesday.

📄 Revise

Modal verbs tell us how likely an action is:

1. Whether someone is able to do something: Isaac **can** play guitar.

2. How likely something is: It **could** rain tomorrow.

They express degrees of certainty.

Must is more certain than **could**.   **Could** is less certain than **will**.

Learn these modal verbs:

We **must** be on time.   I **will** run quickly.   We **could** go swimming.

✔ Skills Check

1. **Underline the modal verbs in this sentence.**

   We could stay in on Saturday night but we might go to the cinema instead.

2. **Choose the best modal verb to fit in this sentence.**

   George ___MUST___ improve his backhand if he wants to win the tennis match.

3. **Which of these events is most likely to happen?**

   Tick one.   Emma will buy some jeans on Saturday. ☑

   Emma should buy some jeans on Saturday. ☐

   Emma ought to buy some jeans on Saturday. ☐

KEY WORDS
auxiliary verbs
modal verbs

11

Adverbs

What is an adverb?

↻ Recap

An **adverb** describes a verb. It tells us how something is done.

📄 Revise

Adverbs give us more detail about a verb.
Adverbs often go next to the verb, but may go somewhere else in the sentence.

It snowed. The sentence tells us it snowed, but not *how* it snowed!

It snowed **softly**.

It snowed **heavily**.

It snowed **silently**.

These **adverbs** describe the verb **snowed**.
Adverbs often end in **ly**. Each adverb changes *how* it snowed.

Adverbs describe the verb. They often end in ly.

✔ Skills Check

1. **Circle the adverbs in each sentence.**

   a. He gently stroked the frightened kitten.

   b. They ran desperately to catch the train.

2. **Write a suitable adverb for each sentence.**

   a. She _calmly_ opened the enormous parcel.

   b. We _carfully_ searched the gloomy forest.

KEY WORD

adverbs

Adverbs and adverbials of time, place and manner

What is an adverbial phrase?

↺ Recap

An **adverbial phrase** tells us how, where or when something happened.

🗏 Revise

Here are some examples of different types of adverb.
An adverbial phrase tells us:

- *how* it was done (manner) – **They climbed** with great determination.
- *where* it was done (place) – **The letter was posted** through the letter-box.
- *when* it was done (time) – **She read her book** before tea.

Be careful! Some words may be prepositions, such as back or up. Some words can also be **adjectives**, such as slow. Check how the word is used.

Adverbs of time	Adverbs of place	Adverbs of manner
during	above	some adverbs ending **ly**, such as angrily, carefully, accidentally
afterwards	abroad	wide
sometimes	behind	late
rarely	nowhere	fast
recently	west	slow
usually	indoors	well
frequently	towards	hard
today	over	
never	nearby	

KEY WORD
adverbials

✔ Skills Check

1. Tick the correct box to show the type of adverb for each word in bold.

Sentence	Adverb of time	Adverb of place	Adverb of manner
Rarely has the show been so successful.	✓		
She practised **hard** for the piano test.			✓
They didn't know the treasure was **nearby**.		✓	

Adverbs of possibility

↺ Recap

What is an adverb of possibility?

An adverb of possibility shows how certain we are about something.

These adverbs of possibility show we are sure of something happening:

definitely   **certainly**   **obviously**   **clearly**

These adverbs of possibility show we are less sure of something happening:

probably   **perhaps**   **maybe**   **possibly**

📄 Revise

Maybe and **perhaps** usually come at the **beginning** of a sentence or clause.

> **Perhaps** there will be ice cream for tea.
> **Maybe** I can have a tablet for my birthday.

Other adverbs of possibility usually come in front of the main verb.

> It is **clearly** going to rain.

However, they come after the verbs **am**, **is**, **are**, **was** and **were**.

> It is **certainly** a busy road.

✔ Skills check

1. **Choose the best adverb of possibility for each sentence.**

   a. It is ___certenly___ six miles to town.   **b.** I can ___certenly___ come to see you later.

   c. ___Perhaps___ we can have tea together?

2. **Explain how each adverb of possibility changes the meaning of the sentences below.**

   We are clearly going to win this game.   We are possibly going to win this game.

   ___One shows that they will and___
   ___the other shows that they might___

14

Fronted adverbials

⟳ Recap

> **What is a fronted adverbial?**

A **fronted adverbial** is an adverb or an adverbial phrase which is at the beginning of a sentence.

Fronted adverbials are usually followed by a comma.

🗏 Revise

After the rain, we were delighted to see a magnificent rainbow.

Adverbial phrase at the beginning of the sentence.
Adverbial of time describes *when* they can see the rainbow.

rest of sentence

KEY WORD
fronted adverbials

Sadly, they packed their belongings and returned home.

Adverb of manner,
also a fronted adverbial.

rest of sentence

In the water, they were surrounded by an abundance of coloured fish.

Adverbial of place describes *where* there were fish.

rest of sentence

> A **fronted adverbial** comes at the front of the sentence. An adverbial phrase can come anywhere in the sentence.

✔ Skills Check

1. **Rewrite the sentence below so it begins with a fronted adverbial. Use only the same words and remember to punctuate your sentence correctly.**

   The puppies played happily in the garden.

   _____

2. **Replace the fronted adverbial in this sentence.**

   Despite the traffic, they arrived at the party early.

   _____

Clauses

↺ Recap

What is a clause?

A **clause** is a group of words which contain a subject (a person or thing who does the verb) and verb.

📄 Revise

> A clause must have a subject and a verb. A clause makes sense, but may be dependent on other parts of the sentence.

The campsite was full.

↑

A clause can be a complete sentence.
It has a subject (**the campsite**) and a verb (**was**).
A sentence can have more than one clause.

The campsite was full **because** it was a bank holiday.

↑   ↑   ↑

first clause   **conjunction**   **second clause**

Often clauses aren't sentences, but they must have a subject and a verb.

in the garden   they **played** in the garden

↑   ↑   ↖

no verb so not a clause   subject: they   verb: played – it's a clause!

✔ Skills Check

1. Tick the correct box to show if each group of words is a clause.

Group of words	Clause	Not a clause
they came home	✓	
because they		✓
it was a wonderful beach holiday	✓	

2. **Underline the clause in each sentence.**

   a. Despite the long delay, they arrived on time.

   b. They studied hard for their test.

KEY WORD

clauses

Main and subordinate clauses

↻ Recap

What are the different types of clause?

A **main clause** is an independent clause that makes sense by itself.

A **subordinate clause** is dependent on the main clause to make sense.

📋 Revise

Ranvir was late for school.

A **main clause** can be a complete sentence as long as it has a subject (**Ranvir**) and a verb (**was**).

Ranvir was late for school **because** the alarm didn't wake her.

↑ main clause   ↑ conjunction   ↑ subordinate clause
Tells us *why* Ranvir was late for school.
Does not make sense by itself.

Even though it was very cold, they went for a long walk.

↗ conjunction   ↑ subordinate clause   ↖ main clause

conjunction

subordinate clause
Can come first.
Does not make sense by itself.

main clause
Does not have to come first.
Makes sense by itself.

KEY WORDS
main clause
subordinate clause

✔ Skills Check

1. Write a main clause for these sentences.

   I am going to go fossil hunting in the evening.

   I know all the steps, although I can't make one.

2. Write a subordinate clause to complete these sentences.

   a. I watched television until _I fell asleep_.

   b. We haven't got much bread though _we ~~should~~ have_.

Co-ordinating conjunctions

↻ Recap

A **co-ordinating conjunction** joins two clauses which would make sense on their own.

📄 Revise

An easy way to remember the co-ordinating conjunctions: the initial letters spell **fanboys!**

The co-ordinating conjunctions are:

| for | and | nor | but | or | yet | so |

co-ordinating conjunction
↓
The magician waved his wand **but the spell didn't work.**
↖ ↗
Each part of the sentence makes sense by itself.

co-ordinating conjunction
↓
He spent several hours learning his spellings **yet he didn't get them all right.**
↖ ↗
Each part makes sense.

✔ Skills Check

KEY WORD
co-ordinating conjunctions

1. Choose the best conjunction for each sentence.

| nor | but | so |

a. My new bike was light ___so___ I was able to go very fast.

b. I like curry ___but___ I don't like it very spicy.

c. I wasn't able to score a goal ___nor___ was I able to help my team score.

2. Join these sentences using the same conjunction.

a. I wanted a new tablet ___but___ they were very expensive.

b. The house was very cold ___but___ the central heating was on.

Subordinating conjunctions

What is a subordinating conjunction?

↻ Recap

A **subordinating conjunction** introduces a subordinate clause, which is dependent on the main clause.

Subordinating conjunctions include:

| because | if | when | since |

| before | that | although | though |

| whenever | then | while | unless |

📋 Revise

KEY WORDS
subordinating conjunctions

subordinating conjunction
↓
I can hold the dog **while** you bath it.
↑   ↑
main clause   subordinate clause

subordinating conjunction
↓
I have a snorkel **although** I don't know how to use it!
↑   ↑
main clause   subordinate clause

Remember, a subordinating conjunction introduces a subordinate clause.

✔ Skills Check

1. **Choose a different conjunction to introduce the final clause in each sentence.**

   a. I can't go swimming ___so___ you give me a lift.

   b. I will go out with you ___if___ you are free.

2. **Complete the sentences with a final clause.**

   a. More people came in after ___we went to get water___.

   b. Even though you are my elder sister ___I will not do what you say___.

19

Relative clauses

A **relative clause** is a type of subordinate clause that adds information about a previous noun.
Relative clauses start with a **relative pronoun**:

| that | which | who | whom |

| whose | where | when |

Relative pronouns introduce a relative clause and are used to start a description about a noun.

What is a relative clause?

📄 Revise

KEY WORDS
relative clause
relative pronouns

The **man, whose car it was,** shouted angrily.

↑
Relative clause, starts with **whose**.
Describes what the **man** owned. It modifies the noun.

The **lioness, which was only two years old,** was used to being with people.

↑
Relative clause, starts with **which**.
Describes the **lioness**. It describes the noun.

Relative clauses are often enclosed by commas. They start with a relative pronoun.

✔ Skills Check

1. Write a relative clause for these sentences.

   a. The hotel, _which was rated 5-star_, was next to the beach.

   b. August, _which is in summer_, is very busy.

2. Put a tick to show the type of clause for the words in bold.

Sentence	Main clause	Subordinate clause	Relative clause
The rain, **which fell heavily**, made us cancel the trip.		✓	✓
We called at Tomas's house **after we had seen Josh.**		✓	
Unless you are able to pay tomorrow, **the trip will be full.**		✓	

Personal and possessive pronouns

↻ Recap

A **pronoun** replaces a noun. There are different types of pronoun. **Personal** and **possessive pronouns** are used to replace people or things.

What is a pronoun?

目 Revise

The personal pronouns are: I you she he it we they

I wiped **the table** and put knives and forks on **it**.

The table is replaced by the **pronoun it** in the second clause.

Jamil and I were travelling by bus and **we** had a long journey.

Jamil and I is replaced by the pronoun **we** in the second clause.

There are also the possessive pronouns: mine yours hers his its ours theirs

These stickers are **mine**.

The **pronoun mine** is used to show possession of the stickers by **me**.

KEY WORDS
pronouns
personal pronouns
possessive pronouns

Using pronouns helps us to avoid repetition.

💡 Tips

male name ➡ male pronoun	
he	his

female name ➡ female pronoun	
she	hers

neutral (not male or female)	
it	its

plural names ➡ plural pronoun /objects	
they	theirs

✔ Skills Check

1. Use the correct pronouns in each sentence.

   a. Alicia enjoyed the party but ___she___ didn't like the food.

   b. George and Oscar went sledging which

   ___they___ found enthralling.

2. Underline the word or words to which each pronoun in bold refers.

   a. I have never used my fountain pen as **it** is too messy!

   b. John and I both devoured **our** food.

Prepositions

What is a preposition?

↺ Recap

A **preposition** links nouns, pronouns or a noun phrase to another word or phrase in the sentence.

KEY WORD
prepositions

📄 Revise

Here are some common prepositions:

about	above	across	after	around	as	at	before
behind	below	beneath	beside	between	by	for	from
in	in front of	inside	into	of	off	on	onto
out of	outside	over	past	under	up	upon	with

Prepositions often tell us the position of a person or object.

The **burglar** squeezed **between** the fence panels.

Preposition between describes the position of the **burglar**.

The **car** was **in front of** the garage.

Preposition in front of describes the position of the **car**.

Prepositions can also be about time.

I went to the newsagents **before** school.
We don't finish school **until** 3.30.

✔ Skills Check

Prepositions should not go at the end of a sentence!

1. **Choose the best preposition for each sentence.**

   out of   without   around

   a. The hawk circled ___around___ its prey.   **b.** He took the milk ___out of___ the fridge.

2. **Write a sentence using each preposition.**

   beneath   across

   The trapdoor was beneath the chair we and in it was a room to located across it.

Determiners

What is a determiner?

↺ Recap

A **determiner** is used to define an object or person (a noun).

📋 Revise

Let's look at the different types of determiner.

Articles	Quantifiers	Demonstratives	Possessives
the, a, an	All numbers: one, two... Ordinals: first, second... many, some, every, any	this, those, these	my, your, our, his her, their

These are just some examples – there are others.

I picked **some** apples from **the** tree and gave them to **my** mother.

↑ quantifier ↑ article ↑ possessive

Each determiner defines the noun that follows it:
some apples (not many or lots of)
my mother (not anyone else's)

You don't need to know the names of each type of determiner but it might help to be aware of them.

✔ Skills check

1. **Choose the best determiner for each sentence. Use each determiner once.**

   our   some   my   the

   a. I washed __my__ face with __the__ soap.

   b. We climbed up __the__ stairs and reached __our__ bedrooms.

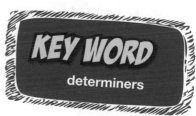

KEY WORD

determiners

2. **Circle each determiner in this sentence.**

   (Every) child must pay (some) money for (the) school trip.

Subjects and objects

↻ Recap

What are subjects and objects?

Every sentence has a **subject**. The subject is the person or thing that does the action of the verb.

Many sentences have objects as well. The **object** has the action of the verb done to it.

Objects are usually nouns, pronouns or noun phrases.

📄 Revise

Let's look at an example.

I am selling.

This sentence has a subject but not an object.
The verb is selling. I am doing the selling. I is the **subject**.

I am selling **my bike**.

In this sentence:
I am still doing the selling so I is still the **subject**.
My bike is being sold. It is having the action of the verb done to it, so **my bike** is the **object**.

In a sentence:

• subjects usually come before the verb

• objects usually come after the verb.

Subject

FOR SALE

Object

KEY WORDS

subject
object

✔ Skills Check

1. **Circle the subject in each of these sentences.**

   a. My mum drove the car.

   b. Our cat ate its food.

2. **Circle the object in each of these sentences.**

   a. Dad is making tea.

   b. The dog chased the cat.

Remember, subjects usually come before the verb. Objects usually come after the verb.

Active and passive verbs

What are active and passive verbs?

↻ **Recap**

Active and **passive** verbs are different forms of verbs.

▤ Revise

Most sentences use the **active** form of a verb. This means that the **subject** is doing the action and the **object** has the action done to it.

KEY WORDS

active voice
passive voice

Kelly scored all three **goals.**

Kelly has done the scoring so she is the **subject**.

The **goals** do not do the scoring. They have been scored so they are the **object.**

When the **passive** is used, the object moves to the front of the sentence and becomes the subject. The original subject moves to the end of the sentence but does not become the object. It becomes part of a **prepositional phrase**.

All three goals were scored by **Kelly.**

All three goals has moved to the front of the sentence and becomes the subject.

Kelly has moved to the end of the sentence.

The passive form can be used in formal writing.

To recognise the passive, look at the end of the sentence. It usually has **by** someone or something after the verb.

✔ Skills Check

1. **Put a tick in the correct box to show whether each sentence is active or passive.**

Sentence	Active	Passive
The winning shot was made by Alisha.		✓
The team won the league.	✓	
Small mammals are hunted by eagles.		✓
Many people have climbed Mount Everest.	✓	

2. **Rewrite this sentence in the passive form.**

The chef made a wonderful meal.

_____

Subjunctive

What is the subjunctive?

📄 Revise

The subjunctive uses only the simple form of a verb. For example, the simple form of **to run** is **run**.

The word **that** will help you to recognise the subjunctive. If the verb can be followed by **that** and something **should** happen, you will be using the subjunctive:

> I demand that you be quiet.

Subjunctives are used in different ways:

- **verb + that**   to advise that   to ask that   to command that

  to demand that   to insist that   to propose that   to recommend that

  to request that   to suggest that

- **after phrases + that**   it is essential that   it is desirable that   it is vital that

- **I, he or she + were:** It is more natural to write **if I was to go to**, but this would be informal. The subjunctive form would be **if I were to go to**. This is known as the past subjunctive.

- **verb + that + be**   I insist that you be here.

✔ Skills Check

Subjunctives are only used in formal speech or writing. They are often used to suggest urgency or importance.

1. **Add the subjunctive form of the verb in each sentence.**

   a. It is important that you _are_ on time for the show.

   b. If I _were_ you, I would take the risk.

2. **Underline the subjunctive in these sentences.**

   a. If <u>I</u> were to give you £25, what would you do with it?

   b. The teacher <u>asked</u> that her students be quieter.

KEY WORD

subjunctive

Sentence types: statements and questions

What are the sentence types?

↺ **Recap**

There are four types of **sentence**: **statements**, **questions**, **exclamations** and **commands**.

KEY WORDS

sentence
statement
question
exclamation
command

📄 Revise

All sentences start with a capital letter.

A **statement**: states a fact and ends with a full stop.

> Dubai has a very busy airport.
> My teacher, Mr Smith, is an accomplished pianist.

Both state a fact and end with a full stop = **statements**.

A **question**: asks a question and ends with a question mark.

> Where are you going?
> Which event is most likely to happen?

Both ask a question and end with a question mark = **questions**.

💡 Tips

Questions often start with a question word:

who	why
what	which
where	when

They all start with **wh!**

Remember though that questions may start with other words.

✔ Skills check

1. **Draw lines to join each sentence to the correct label.**

Sentence		Label
It is a sunny day.		statement
Is it sunny?		
What time does it start?		
We can start it soon.		question

2. **Write a question starting with the word below.**

When _did you see it?_

Sentence types: exclamations and commands

 Revise

A command: tells someone to do something and can sometimes end with an exclamation mark.

It is sometimes called an imperative sentence.

No parking!   Line up!

Both are forceful **commands** and need an exclamation mark.

Please do not park here.   ⟵   This is not forceful. It is just a polite request. An exclamation mark is not needed.

An exclamation: expresses excitement, emotion or surprise and ends with an exclamation mark.

How marvellous!   What a terrifying tornado!

Expresses pleasure or excitement.   Expresses surprise or fear.
Both are **exclamations** and end with an exclamation mark.

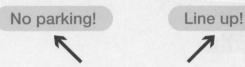

Try saying a sentence. Think about what type of sentence it is. Are you asking a question? Do you need to sound forceful or surprised?

✔ Skills Check

1. Put a tick in the correct column to show the sentence type.

Sentence	Statement	Question	Exclamation	Command
Do you want a new bicycle		✓		
Racing bikes are very aerodynamic	✓			
What an amazing bicycle			✓	
Ride this bike				✓

2. Write an exclamation starting with the word below.

How _____

28

Question tags

What are question tags?

↻ Recap

Question tags come at the end of a sentence. They try to make you agree with the sentence.

📄 Revise

Examples of question tags include: isn't it? don't you? wouldn't you?

They are called **question tags** because they are tagged onto the end of a sentence. They make statements into questions.

You all want to go on the trip.

↑

statement

You all want to go on the trip, **don't you?**

↗

The question tag makes this into a question.

Not all question tags are negative.

No one wants to miss the trip, **do they?**

means the same as

You all want to go on the trip, **don't you?**

↑

positive question tag

↑

negative question tag

A question tag always comes after a comma.

✔ Skills Check

Question tags are easy, aren't they?

1. **Underline the question tags in these sentences.**

   a. You won't be late, <u>will you</u>?

   b. We're going to the cinema, aren't we?

2. **Add appropriate question tags to these sentences.**

   a. You'd like pizza for tea, _don't you_ ?

   b. This is the right answer, _isn't it_ ?

Apostrophes: contraction

What is an apostrophe for contraction?

↻ Recap

An **apostrophe** for **contraction** is a punctuation mark used to show where letters have been missed out when two words are joined.

🗒 Revise

We use the apostrophe to show where letters have been missed out.

I am = I'm
↑
missing letter – **a**

they could/they had = they'd
↑
missing letters – **coul/ha**

we are = we're
↑
missing letter – **a**

did not = didn't
↑
missing letter – **o**

The apostrophe must replace the missing letter or letters in the same place.

💡 Tip

Here are some common contractions:

you are	→	you're
there is	→	there's
was not	→	wasn't
could not	→	couldn't
have not	→	haven't
she will	→	she'll
could have	→	could've
they have	→	they've
I would	→	I'd
John is	→	John's

Exception to the rule:
will not → won't

When looking at a contraction, ask yourself which letters have been missed out. Where should the apostrophe go?

✔ Skills Check

1. Circle the correct contraction in each sentence.
   a. I wonder if **itl'l** / **it'll** / **i'tll** be sunny later.
   b. I **shouldve'** / **shouldv'e** / **should've** sent a birthday card to my gran.

2. Write the correct contraction for these words.
   a. had not   *hadn't*
   b. could have *could've*
   c. we would   *we'd wed*

Apostrophes: possession

What is an apostrophe for possession?

↻ Recap

An **apostrophe** and the letter **s** are often used to show **possession**; to show when an object belongs to someone or something.

📄 Revise

To use an apostrophe to show possession, you need to know if the possessor of the object is **singular** or **plural**. This will help you decide where to put the apostrophe.

Single possessor

the car's headlights
one car: **apostrophe + s**

the frog's lilypad
one frog: **apostrophe + s**

this week's work
one week: **apostrophe + s**

Plural possessors

the cars' headlights
several cars: **s + apostrophe**

the frogs' lilypad
several frogs: **s + apostrophe**

several weeks' work
several weeks: **s + apostrophe**

KEY WORDS

apostrophe
possession
singular
plural

Check how many possessors are there?
One possessor = apostrophe + s
Several possessors = s + apostrophe

💡 Tips

Before adding an apostrophe, be sure that you need to show possession.

The men enjoyed the game.
↖
Several men – no possession.

The men's game was enjoyable.
↖
The game belongs to the men – possession.

✔ Skills Check

1. **Rewrite each phrase using apostrophes to show possession.**

   a. The bags belong to the girls.

   Those are the girls' bags.

   b. The crayons belong to the boy.

   ~~Those are the girls'~~
   That is the boy's crayons.

2. **Insert an apostrophe into the correct place in the underlined word.**

   The <u>trains'</u> arrivals were all delayed by the weather.

Commas in lists

How are commas used in lists?

↻ Recap

A **comma** is a punctuation mark that can be used to separate items in a list.

📋 Revise

Don't use a comma if there are only two items in the list.

> I bought some bread and cheese.　　two items: no comma needed

If you have more than two items in a list, use commas.

> I bought some bread, cheese, grapes **and** chutney.

Use commas to separate each item.　　Use **and** before the last item.

> We went to Rome, Venice, Sorrento, Pisa **and** the Italian Lakes.

Use a comma after each item.　　Do not use a comma before **and**.

KEY WORD
comma

✔ Skills check

1. Insert commas in the correct places in these sentences.

   a. We had Jack Amir Rashid and Josef on our team.

   b. The children enjoyed their picnic of sausage rolls egg sandwiches apples crisps and juice.

2. Tick the sentence which uses commas correctly.

   Europe is made up of many countries including Britain, France Spain Germany, and Italy. ☐

   Europe is made up of many countries including Britain, France, Spain Germany and, Italy. ☐

   Europe is made up of many countries including Britain, France, Spain, Germany and Italy. ☐

Commas to separate clauses

How do commas separate clauses?

↺ Recap

Commas can be used to divide clauses to make sentences easier to understand.

📋 Revise

Main clause and subordinate clause

I made tea **while** Asha set the table.

subordinating conjunction

subordinate clause at the end of the sentence: **no comma**

While Asha set the table, I made tea.

subordinating conjunction

subordinate clause at the start of the sentence: **comma always used**

Main clause and relative clause

relative pronoun

Cherry passed the ball to Donna, **who** scored easily.

relative clause: **comma usually used**

Clauses in the middle of a sentence

Sometimes the main clause is split by another clause.

main clause

Dev, **who is the best runner in the school,** won the county championship.

comma to separate clauses   relative clause   comma to separate clauses

✔ Skills Check

1. Insert commas into the correct places to separate the clauses.

   a. My favourite city is Paris which is the capital of France.

   b. Paris which is my favourite city is the capital of France.

Commas to clarify meaning

↺ Recap

How are commas used to clarify meaning?

Commas are be placed in sentences to help us understand the meaning. Using commas within a sentence can help make the meaning clearer and avoid ambiguity.

🗒 Revise

Sometimes the meaning isn't clear without commas.

In the following sentences the words are the same but the comma makes the meaning different:

"Let's eat Dad."

"Let's eat, Dad."

Someone is suggesting we should eat Dad!

That's clearer. Someone is telling Dad to eat.

The comma alters the meaning.

In the next two sentences, the commas alter the meaning again.

"My grandad in the distance could see a car." ← My grandad is in the distance and could see a car.

"My grandad, in the distance, could see a car." ← My grandad could see a car in the distance.

✔ Skills Check

1. Put commas in the correct places to make the meaning clear.

  a. My mum loves cooking my dad and me.

  b. Nate invited two boys John and Eddy.

  c. My uncle a singer and a dancer often appeared on television.

  d. Has the cat eaten Callum?

Commas after fronted adverbials

↺ Recap

What are commas after fronted adverbials?

A **fronted adverbial** is an adverb or an adverbial phrase, which is at the beginning of a sentence. A fronted adverbial is always followed by a comma.

Revise

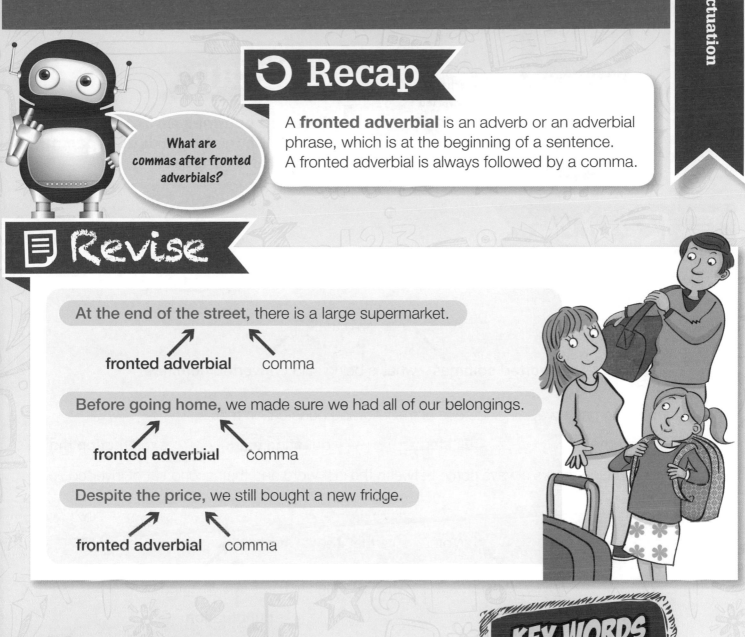

At the end of the street, there is a large supermarket.

fronted adverbial   comma

Before going home, we made sure we had all of our belongings.

fronted adverbial   comma

Despite the price, we still bought a new fridge.

fronted adverbial   comma

KEY WORDS
fronted adverbials

✔ Skills Check

1. Place commas in the correct places in these sentences.

a. Grim and sinister the graveyard lay before me.

b. After lunch we had geography and art.

c. Patiently I waited my turn.

d. While the lead singer sang loudly the guitarist played the backing tune.

e. Silently and softly the snow fell outside.

f. Running to catch the bus I tripped and fell.

2. Write your own fronted adverbial for this sentence. Remember to punctuate it correctly.

_____ it was a wonderful barbeque.

Inverted commas

What are inverted commas?

Inverted commas are also called 'speech marks'. They go around **direct speech** to show what is being said.

📄 Revise

Inverted commas go at the beginning and end of speech.

"Who said that?"

inverted commas   what is being said   **inverted commas**

Inverted commas *always* include one of the following punctuation marks:

| comma | full stop | question mark | exclamation mark |

The punctuation marks always come between the last word and the second set of inverted commas.

"I'm pretty sure that it was Christine!"

inverted commas   what is being said   inverted commas

punctuation

A **comma** is used when the writing continues past the end of the speech.

"You need to be able to use commas properly," said Mum. "They help you clarify meaning."

A **full stop** is only used when the speech is the end of the writing.
In this case, the comma moves in front of the first set of inverted commas.

Mum said, "You need to be able to use commas properly. They help you clarify meaning."

Question marks and **exclamation marks** are used in the same way depending upon the sentence types.

Mum said, "Why do you need to be able to use commas properly?"

Mum said, "You need to be able to use commas properly!"

KEY WORDS
direct speech
inverted commas

✔ Skills Check

1. Place inverted commas in the correct places in the following sentences.

   a. We can sit over there, said Demi.

   b. Sherri said, This punctuation stuff is easy.

2. Add the correct punctuation marks to the following sentences.

   a. Donny said " I like eating cream cakes "

   b. " They're not good for you " replied Shirley.

3. Rewrite the following sentences so that the words that are spoken come at the end of the sentences. An example has been done for you.

"We are going to the beach today," said Jerry.

Jerry said, "We are going to the beach today."

a. "On Sunday we are going to Nan's for tea," said my sister.

_____

b. "This bus is going to town," said the driver.

_____

💡 Tips

- Everything that is being said *and* a punctuation mark goes inside the inverted commas.
- Make sure you use the correct punctuation mark *before* the second set of inverted commas.

Remember the comma after words like **said** when you are using inverted commas.

37

Colons and semi-colons

↻ Recap

What are colons and semi-colons?

Colons (:) and **semi-colons** (;) are punctuation marks that are used within sentences to separate ideas.

Colons:
- introduce lists, summaries, examples and quotations
- mark the boundary between two independent clauses.

Semi-colons:
- show a link between two ideas
- separate complicated items within a list
- mark the boundary between two independent clauses.

▤ Revise

Colons

Here are some examples of how colons introduce lists, summaries, examples and quotations.

List – To build this model tree you will need: glue, scissors, a ruler, tissue paper and some wire.

Summary – We have learnt the following: deciduous trees lose their leaves in winter.

Example – Examples of deciduous trees are: oak, sycamore, chestnut and poplar.

Quotation – Shakespeare wrote: "Under the greenwood tree, who loves to lie with me… Here shall he see no enemy but winter and rough weather."

Colons also mark the boundary between two independent clauses which make sense by themselves:

The weather was awful this weekend: it rained all Saturday and Sunday.

Semi-colons

Here is an example of how a semi-colon can show a link between two ideas.

Petrol is a fuel for cars; so is diesel.

Semi-colons also separate complicated items within a list.

I had to buy some garlic paste and tomatoes from the deli; some onions and potatoes from the grocer; and some plastic plates from the hardware shop.

As with colons, semi-colons mark the boundary between two independent clauses, but when the second part is related to the first part.

The weather was awful this weekend; I knew it would be.

✔ Skills check

1. Insert colons in the correct places.

a. You will need to bring with you your passport, plane tickets, money, sun cream and sunglasses.

b. We now know some countries that border the Mediterranean Sea Egypt, France, Spain and Italy.

c. Warm waters can be found in the Mediterranean Sea, the Caribbean Sea and the Indian Ocean.

d. In *Julius Caesar*, Shakespeare wrote "There is a tide in the affairs of men. Which, taken at the flood, leads on to fortune."

e. Phoebe often wears sunglasses the bright light hurts her eyes.

2. Insert a semi-colon to link the two ideas.

May has thirty days so does June.

3. Rewrite this bullet-point list as a sentence.

I need to go to
* the supermarket for some dog food
* the heel bar where my shoes have been mended
* the library to get some books for my history project.

Remember, colons and semi-colons are links. They go before the second part of a sentence.

_____

_____

_____

4. Insert a semi-colon to mark the boundary between the two independent clauses.

Water boils at 100 degrees Celsius at sea level it freezes at 0 degrees.

Parenthesis

What is parenthesis?

↻ Recap

Parenthesis is the term used for a word, clause or phrase that is inserted into a sentence to provide more detail.
- Parenthesis is what is written inside **brackets**.
- **Commas** and **dashes** can do the same job as brackets.

Revise

KEY WORDS
parenthesis
brackets
commas
dashes

Parenthesis does not make any difference to the understanding of the original sentence. It just gives the reader more information.

The following sentence gives a piece of information:

> The Eiffel Tower is a very tall building.

By adding parenthesis, more detail is given but the meaning remains the same:

> The Eiffel Tower (which is in Paris) is a very tall building.

parenthesis with brackets

Commas and pairs of dashes can do the same job as brackets:

> The Eiffel Tower, which is in Paris, is a very tall building.

parenthesis with commas

> The Eiffel Tower – which is in Paris – is a very tall building.

parenthesis with dashes

Dashes tend to be used in less formal writing, such as in an email.

Remember, parenthesis is the information you add, not the punctuation around it.

✔ Skills check

1. a. Insert the parenthesis into the following sentence, using brackets.

The three men talked quietly in the corner of the cafe. **Parenthesis:** *they looked like spies to me*

_____

b. Insert the parenthesis into the following sentence, using commas.

Denny is joining the army. **Parenthesis:** *my older brother*

_____

c. Insert the parenthesis into the following sentence, using dashes.

Suki won first prize at the dog show. **Parenthesis:** *a long-haired Alsatian*

_____

d. Insert the parenthesis into the following sentence, using either brackets, commas or dashes.

I had to keep very still while the doctor took my stitches out.
Parenthesis: *who was very gentle*

_____

e. Insert Parenthesis 1 and Parenthesis 2 into the correct places in the following sentence, using dashes and commas.

The strongest wind ever will hit this country.
Parenthesis 1: *A massive hurricane*
Parenthesis 2: *probably on Tuesday next week*

_____

_____

Hyphens

What is a hyphen?

Recap

Hyphens are punctuation marks that are used to:

- join words together
- clarify meaning
- help pronunciation
- follow some prefixes.

Don't confuse hyphens and dashes. Dashes are longer and are used for parenthesis.

Revise

Sometimes we join words together using a hyphen to show that they are linked.

It was a **low-budget** film.

In this sentence, the film is neither low nor budget. We have to link the two words together to get low-budget, meaning it did not cost much.

The meaning of some sentences isn't clear without a hyphen.

Joe Montana was a famous American football player.

The sentence is ambiguous. Was Joe a famous American who played football, or was he famous for playing American football? Adding a hyphen shows that Joe played American football.

Joe Montana was a famous **American-football** player.

Without a hyphen, we would not know how to pronounce words like **re-enter**. The hyphen tells us that the letters on either side of it are both pronounced.

Here are some examples of when hyphens follow prefixes.

ex-police officer   **all-**inclusive   **self-**conscious

Skills Check

KEY WORD
hyphen

1. **Insert hyphens to join the correct words together.**

   My mother in law is coming for Sunday lunch.

2. **Insert a hyphen in this sentence to make it clear that the instruments have not been used much.**

   My uncle, a retired surgeon, showed me some of his little used instruments.

3. **Rewrite 'resign' with a hyphen to show that it means 'to sign again'.**

   ____

Ellipsis

What is ellipsis?

↻ Recap

Ellipsis is the omission of repeated, predictable or unnecessary words.

📄 Revise

Imagine this question has been asked: "Where are you going?"

This is the reply: "I'm going to the skate park."

Not every word of the reply is necessary. It could just have been "To the skate park." or even "The skate park."

Sometimes words are repeated in a response. "Who was the prime minster in 1943?

"The prime minster in 1943 was Winston Churchill." could just have been

"Winston Churchill."

In this sentence, 'some' has been repeated when it doesn't need to be.
We have bought some apples, some oranges, some bananas and some pears.

The sentence could be: We have bought some apples, oranges, bananas and pears.

✔ Skills Check

KEY WORD

ellipsis

1. **Underline the unnecessary words.**

   a. My son was born at the start of this century, in 2001.

   b. I went because I wanted to go.   **c.** My sister likes salad but I don't like salad.

2. **Insert the words that are missing.**

   a. "Do you want to go to the park?"   "_____ we don't."

   b. "Have you finished your homework?"   "_____ I have.

   c. "Who does the cooking in your house?"   "My dad _____."

43

Paragraphs

What are paragraphs?

↻ Recap

Paragraphs organise writing to make it easier to understand.
- They break text down into small sections so it is easy to read.
- They are a series of sentences about the same idea.
- We start a new paragraph for each different idea, place, time, character or event.

Revise

In the following story, Arty is a police officer.

> A shiver ran down Arty's spine. Night observations. She hated them. She was always scared because she never knew how they would turn out.

new paragraph for a new idea

> She heard footsteps approaching from her right-hand side. It was Ben, Arty's work partner, who had been checking out the other end of the street.

new paragraph   different idea   different event

> It was time to move. Together they crept from their hiding place towards the warehouse, which lay before them, dim, dark and threatening.

new paragraph   different place   different character

> Inside the warehouse, Jim Evans and three of his gang were loading up a van.

✔ Skills Check

1. **Draw two lines (//) to show where a new paragraph should begin. Give a reason for your answer.**

   Jim Evans was a small-time crook who made his money by selling stolen goods. He had often been in trouble with the law. Outside the warehouse, Arty and Ben waited patiently for back-up. They knew they couldn't do this alone.

   Reason: _____

Headings and subheadings

> What are headings and subheadings?

↻ Recap

Headings are titles for pieces of writing – they go at the start of the piece.

Subheadings are titles for sections of writing within a longer piece – they go at the start of the section.

- They make the writing easier to read by structuring it.
- They often summarise the writing.

📄 Revise

Surfing!	⟵	**Heading** – tells us what the whole piece is about.
Basic equipment	⟵	**Subheading** – gives a summary of this section.

It's exciting and dangerous but surfing is growing in popularity. If you want to try it, there are two things you absolutely have to have: a surf board and big waves. You can do something about the board but you can't do much about the waves!

💡 Tips

The text in a question will normally be more than one paragraph long. **Read all of it** and decide what the **main idea** is. That will be the **heading**. Then try to give **short summaries** of **each section**. These will be the **subheadings**.

✔ Skills Check

1. Read the following text and suggest a heading and a subheading.

a. Heading: _____

Did you know that not everyone speaks like you? I don't mean people in other countries with other languages. I mean here, in Britain. It's really strange, some words are the same but they aren't pronounced anything like each other.

b. Subheading: _____

My cousins, who live a hundred miles away, say "Barth", while I know it should be pronounced "Bath". They say, "scon". Don't they know it's "scone"? They don't say "ston" when they mean "stone".

Synonyms

What are synonyms?

↻ Recap

Synonyms are words with the same or similar meaning.

☰ Revise

Using different synonyms for words can make our writing more interesting.

It is a **big** elephant.

Large, **enormous** and **massive** are all synonyms for big.

"That is an **enormous** elephant," **said** Ranvir.

The word **said** can be changed for a more interesting synonym:

declared spoke uttered pronounced

enormous

BIG

large

massive

💡 Tips

When writing, ask these questions.
• What other words mean the same?
• Are they more interesting or precise?

Can you think of some synonyms?

KEY WORD

synonyms

✔ Skills Check

1. Tick all the synonyms for the word 'difficult'.

complex ☐

arduous ☐

effortless ☐

intricate ☐

easy ☐

2. **Draw lines to match each word to its synonym.**

ancient   genuine

curious   antique

familiar   inquisitive

sincere   known

Antonyms

What is an antonym?

↺ Recap

Antonyms are words with the opposite meaning.

📄 Revise

Light is the antonym of **heavy**. It has the opposite meaning.

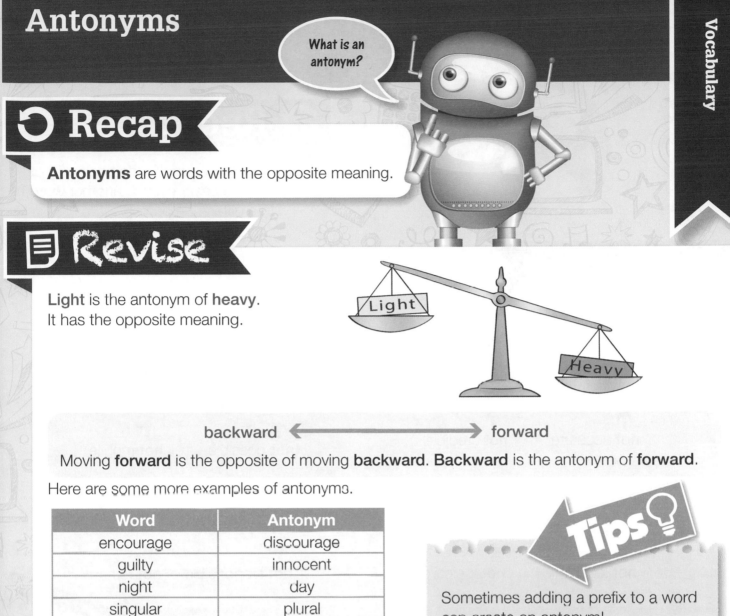

backward ⟷ forward

Moving **forward** is the opposite of moving **backward**. **Backward** is the antonym of **forward**.

Here are some more examples of antonyms.

Word	Antonym
encourage	discourage
guilty	innocent
night	day
singular	plural

Tips 💡

Sometimes adding a prefix to a word can create an antonym!
- happy ⟶ **un**happy
- encourage ⟶ **dis**courage

✔ Skills Check

1. Draw lines to join each word to its antonym.

healthy	minimum
young	mature
permanent	unwell
maximum	temporary

KEY WORD

antonyms

2. Choose an antonym to replace each word in bold.

a. I **made** a massive tower. _____

b. The successful man was very **humble**. _____

c. The **foolish** child had no packed lunch. _____

Prefixes: in or im? il or ir?

What is a prefix?

↻ Recap

A **prefix** is added to the beginning of a word to change it into another word, with a different meaning.

🗒 Revise

Each prefix has a different meaning.

The prefixes **in**, **im**, **il** and **ir** all have negative meanings (they often mean **not**).

inaccurate
↑
not accurate

incredible
↑
not credible

im is used with words beginning with **p** or **m**

impossible
↑
not possible

immobile
↑
not mobile

il goes before words beginning with **l**

illegal
↑
not legal

illogical
↑
not logical

ir goes before words beginning with **r**

irresponsible
↑
not responsible

irretrievable
↑
not retrievable

✔ Skills Check

Tips 💡

1. **Choose the correct prefix to change each word to its opposite meaning.**

   ir   il   im   in

   a. ____mature

   b. ____relevant

   c. ____accessible

   d. ____legible

Think about the letter that the root word starts with.
- **il** = words starting with **l**
- **ir** = words starting with **r**
- **im** = words starting with **p** or **m**

For all other words, try the prefixes **un**, **in**, **dis** or **re**.

2. **Circle the correct use of a prefix in each sentence.**

   a. Emily had several **imcorrect / ilcorrect / incorrect** answers.

   b. They waited **impatiently / inpatiently / irpatiently** to be chosen for the team.

   c. An **ilregular / inregular / irregular** hexagon has six unequal sides.

KEY WORD

prefix

Prefixes: re, dis or mis?

📝 Revise

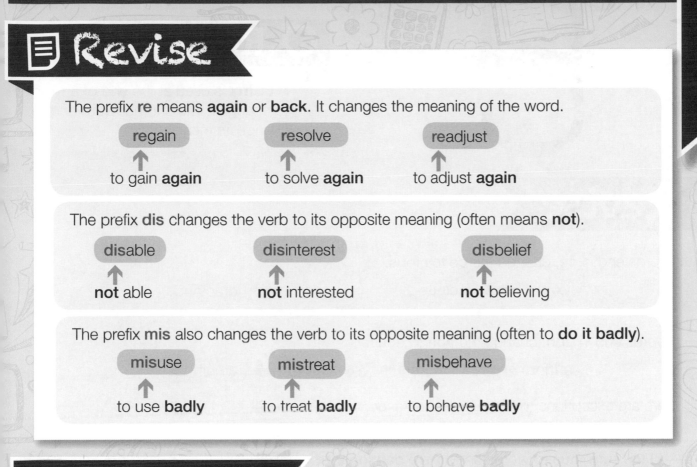

The prefix **re** means **again** or **back**. It changes the meaning of the word.

regain	resolve	readjust
↑	↑	↑
to gain **again**	to solve **again**	to adjust **again**

The prefix **dis** changes the verb to its opposite meaning (often means **not**).

disable	disinterest	disbelief
↑	↑	↑
not able	**not** interested	**not** believing

The prefix **mis** also changes the verb to its opposite meaning (often to **do it badly**).

misuse	mistreat	misbehave
↑	↑	↑
to use **badly**	to treat **badly**	to behave **badly**

✔ Skills check

1. Draw lines to match the prefixes to the root words. Then write each new word.

re   loyal   _____

dis   judge   _____

mis   design   _____

2. Use a prefix to change the meaning of these words so they match their definitions.

Word	New word	Definition
place		to put back again
calculate		to work out wrongly
tasteful		objectionable

Suffixes: ous, cious or tious?

What is a suffix?

↻ Recap

A **suffix** is used at the end of a word, to change it into another word and to change its meaning.

📄 Revise

If words end in **ce**, change the **ce** to **cious**.

vi**ce** → vi**cious**   gra**ce** → gra**cious**

If words end in **tion**, change the **tion** to **tious**.

cau**tion** → cau**tious**   ambi**tion** → ambi**tious**

There are exceptions to this rule. For instance, fic**tion** → fic**titious**

Add the suffix **ous** to words ending in a **consonant**.

dange**r** → dange**rous**   poiso**n** → poiso**nous**

If words end in **our**, change **our** to **or** and then add **ous**.

hum**our** → hum**orous**   glam**our** → glam**orous**

Words ending in **ge** keep **ge** + **ous**.

coura**ge** → coura**geous**   advanta**ge** → advanta**geous**

✔ Skills Check

KEY WORD

suffix

1. Add the correct suffix to make a new word. Write the word.

   ous   cious   tious

   a. malice _____   **c.** vigour_____

   b. infection _____   **d.** mountain _____

2. Circle the correct spelling of each word.

   a. religous / religious / religeous   **b.** consciencious / conscientious / consciencous

Suffixes: ant or ent? ance or ence? ancy or ency?

📋 Revise

To work out which suffix to use it helps to know that some of them are related.

Words ending in **ation** often use the **ant**, **ance** or **ancy** suffixes.

Let's look at some:

hesit**ation** → hesit**ant** → hesit**ance** → hesit**ancy**

They all have **a** in the suffix.

Use **ent**, **ence** or **ency** after a soft **c** sound or after **qu**:

inno**cent** → inno**cence**   fre**quent** → fre**quence** → fre**quency**

Tips 💡

There are words that don't follow these guidelines, which you need to learn.

For example: independ**ent**   assist**ance**

If one of a word's suffixes has an **a** in it, others might: assist**ant**   assist**ance**

✔ Skills Check

1. Choose the correct suffix for each word. Then write out the words in full in the boxes. In some cases none of the suffixes make a word, so some rows should be left blank.

Start of word	ant or ent?	ance or ence?	ancy or ency?
dec			
confid			
toler			
obedi			

2. Circle the correct spelling to complete each sentence.

a. The **non-existance** / **non-existence** of dodos in Mauritius has long been a cause for regret.

b. Your help is more of a **hindrance** / **hindrence**.

c. Please complete the **relevent** / **relevant** application form.

Word families

What is a word family?

📄 Revise

Adding a prefix or suffix will change the meaning of the word and might change its function.

Start with a **root word** and then try adding different prefixes and suffixes. How has the word changed?

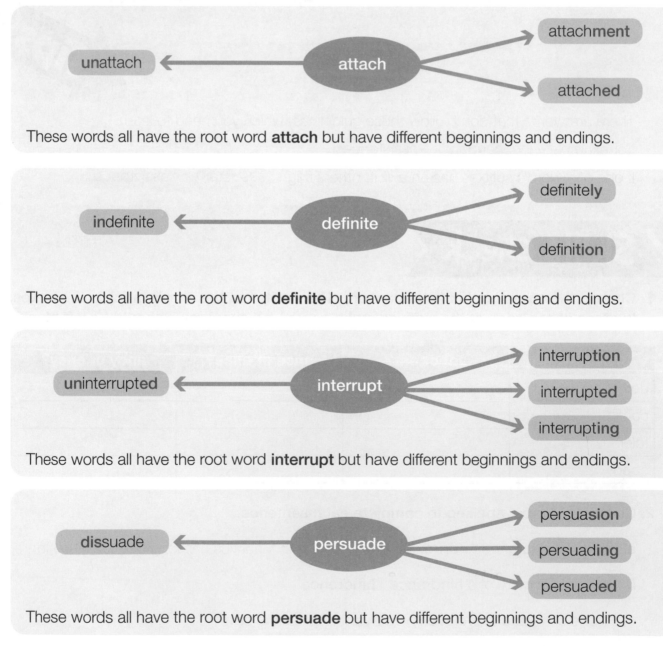

unattach ← attach → attach**ment**

attach**ed**

These words all have the root word **attach** but have different beginnings and endings.

indefinite ← definite → definite**ly**

defin**ition**

These words all have the root word **definite** but have different beginnings and endings.

uninterrupt**ed** ← interrupt → interrup**tion**

interrupt**ed**

interrupt**ing**

These words all have the root word **interrupt** but have different beginnings and endings.

dissuade ← persuade → persua**sion**

persuad**ing**

persuad**ed**

These words all have the root word **persuade** but have different beginnings and endings.

✔ Skills Check

1. **Make word families by adding two suffixes to each root word. Write the new words in full.**

   a. critic _____ _____

   b. depend _____ _____

   c. achieve _____ _____

2. **Split each word into its different parts.**

Word	Root word	Suffix	Prefix
impatience			
unfriendly			
disappointment			

3. **Underline the word which does not belong to each word family.**

   a. unbelievable, disbelief, disembark, believed

   b. redecorate, indecent, decoration, decorated

   c. immaterial, materially, materialise, maternal

If you know a root word and can spell it, you can then make lots of other words, using prefixes and suffixes.

4. **Write the root word used in each of these words.**

   a. disenchantment _____

   b. unenthralling _____

   c. misapplication _____

Always look for the common features to find a word family.

Tips 💡

Sometimes when you add a prefix or suffix to a root word, you need to lose some letters first.
- For words ending in **e**, lose the final **e**.
- Persua**de** + sion: lose **de** and add suffix.

Letter strings: ought

↺ Recap

What is a letter string?

A letter string is a group of letters which make one sound, within a word.

The letters **ought** can be used to make many different sounds.

📄 Revise

These are the most common **ought** words:

ought	thought	bought	brought
sought	fought	nought	wrought

Learn the letter string ought and spelling these words will be easy.

This letter string makes an **ort** sound.

However, in dr**ought** these letters make an **out** sound (as in shout).

✔ Skills check

1. **Choose the best word to go in each sentence.**

   brought   bought   sought   wrought

   a. They _____ a way out of the forest, but it was hard to find.

   b. I _____ some toys with me.

   c. They installed a new _____ iron gate.

   d. We _____ some cakes to have with our sandwiches.

2. **Draw lines to match these words to their definitions.**

ought
fought
nought
thought

nothing
considered
struggled
should

💡 Tips

Be careful: some words have the same sound but are spelled differently, for example **caught** and **court**, **taught** and **taut**.

Letter strings: ough

🔄 Recap

The letter string **ough** makes several sounds: **uff** (as in stuff); **off**; **oo** (as in moon); **oe** (as in toe); and **ow** (as in cow).

What sound does the letter string ough make?

📋 Revise

Using the letter string **ough** can be tricky because it can make so many sounds. Here are some examples of each sound.

uff (as in cuff)	off	oo (as in moon)	oe (as in toe)	ow (as in cow)
rough	cough	through	though	bough
tough	trough		dough	plough

Some **ough** words don't belong in these groups:

thorough   **borough**

These words both have an **uh** sound at the end.

Tips

Say the word, then work out which sound it makes.

✔ Skills Check

1. Use these 'ough' words to make new words to fit in each space.

   dough   **rough**   **tough**

   a. They _____ worked out how to make the model.

   b. The doors were made of _____ glass.

   c. We bought some _____ to eat at the fairground.

2. Write the 'ough' words to match each definition.

Definition	Word
area	
branch	
cultivate	
sufficient	
animal food container	

Silent letters

When are silent letters used?

↻ Recap

Silent letters are used to write a sound – but you can't hear them when you say the word.

🗒 Revise

There are lots of silent letters. They often pair up with another letter:

bt has a silent b

doubt   debt   subtle

↖   ↑   ↗

you only hear the **t** sound

mn has a silent n

solemn   column   autumn

↖   ↑   ↗

you only hear the **m** sound

s can be a silent s

island   aisle   debris

↖   ↑   ↗

you cannot hear the **s** sound

kn has a silent k

knight   knowledge   knit

↖   ↑   ↗

you only hear the **n** sound

st has a silent t

thistle   whistle   castle

↖   ↑   ↗

you only hear the **s** sound

✔ Skills Check

1. **Underline the silent letter in each word in bold.**

   a. They went over the bridge to the **Isle** of Anglesey.

   b. Look at the third **column**.

   c. We are **indebted** to you, thanks to all your efforts.

   d. Caitlin saw a **Mistle** Thrush in the garden.

2. **Circle the correct spelling for each word.**

   a. dought / doubt / dout   c. condam / condemn / condem

   b. isle / iall / iel   d. brissle / brissel / bristle

💡 Tips

To help you spell a word, pronounce it with the silent letter: **sub–tle**.
If you can hear each letter, you will use it when writing the word.

c or s?

What kind of sound can c and s both make?

📄 Revise

How do we know when to use **c** or **s** at the start of a word?

When the next letter is a consonant we must use **s**:

> scrap   smell   snore

When the next letter is **a**, **o** or **u** we must use **s**:

> sanity   sock   Sunday

When the next letter is **e**, **i** or **y** we use **s** or **c**:

> seven   single   synonym
>
> cement   cigar   cygnet

💡 **Tips**

Look out for common word endings using the soft **s** sound:

nce → fence
nce → advance

rce → pierce
rce → resource

After a short vowel sound in short words we use **ss**:   kiss   miss   chess

In longer words we use **ice**: prejudice   precipice   office

face   space   race   all use **ace**.

✔ Skills Check

1. Draw a circle round the correct spelling of the words in bold.

a. I went **twice / twise** to call on Ahmed.

b. There was a very **fierse / fierce** dog behind the gate.

c. It was **bliss / blice** sitting in the hot sun.

d. Our teacher **cuggested / suggested** that we read books by Michael Morpurgo.

2. Write the correct spelling of the word highlighted in bold.

a. Our doctor's **practiss** is very busy. _____

b. I asked for a **peese** of lemon cake. _____

Double trouble

↻ Recap

How do I know when to double letters?

You need to learn when to use double letters and when not to.

double r	double s		no double f	double s

emba**rr**a**ss**   BUT   profe**ss**ion

📄 Revise

Let's look at words with one pair of double letters.

double **r**   double **f**   double **b**

co**rr**espond   di**ff**iculty   bu**bb**le

Learn these words in groups.
It helps you to remember them.

Now let's look at words with two pairs of double letters.

double **g**   double **s**   double **d**   double **s**

a**gg**re**ss**ive   a**dd**re**ss**

Some words even have three pairs of double letters.

double **s** double **s**   double **p**

Mi**ss**i**ss**i**pp**i

💡 Tips

In words of more than one syllable, a double **consonant** usually shows that the **vowel** before it has a short vowel sound. For example: **little**, **misspell**.

✔ Skills Check

1. **Put a tick in the correct column to show the number of pairs of double letters.**

Word	1 pair	2 pairs
guarantee		
accidentally		
pressurised		
immediate		

2. **Write the correct spelling for each definition.**
   Each word has at least one pair of double letters.

   a. To really like something

   _____

   b. A chance to do something

   _____

   c. A decision-making group

   _____

   d. To disrupt a conversation

   _____

Some of the above words can be found in the Year 5–6 word list at the back of the book. Ask an adult to read out some words with double letters and see if you can spell them.

Tricky words

What is a tricky word?

↻ Recap

A tricky word may have:
- several **syllables**
- an unusual spelling pattern.

📄 Revise

You may need to split longer words into parts or syllables to make them easier to spell.

house: 1 syllable

prejudice: 3 syllables

Soft **g** sound: Is it **g** or **j**?   Soft **s** sound: **ice** or **iss**?

- Break the word into syllables (parts).
- Say each part of the word slowly and clearly.
- Then work out how to spell each syllable.

Some words have sounds which could be made in different ways.

Ask: **a** or **e**?   **sion** or **tion**?

explanation – 4 syllables

Try each way. Which looks best?
Say the word clearly and you can hear the **a**.

KEY WORD

syllable

Breaking a word into syllables and then working out how to spell each part makes it easier. Try the different ways of making tricky sounds. Which looks best?

✔ Skills check

1. **Shade each syllable in a different colour. Describe the tricky bits in each word.**

   a. immediately _____

   b. necessary _____

2. **Circle the correct spelling of each word.**

   a. government   goverment   guverment   governmeant

   b. marvelous   marvelus   marvellus   marvellous

   c. wrecognise   reckognise   recognise   reconise

Look at a word you misspell. Write the word correctly. Highlight the tricky bit and memorise the correct spelling.

Homophones

What is a homophone?

↺ Recap

A **homophone** is a pair of words which sound the same but are spelled differently.

📄 Revise

There are lots of homophones. Here are a few examples.

profit ⟶ a financial gain

prophet ⟶ someone who foretells the future

principle ⟶ a belief

principal ⟶ the leader

I awoke early this **morning**.

↗ the start of the day

They are in **mourning** following the king's death.

↗ in sorrow (following a death)

license ⟶ (verb) to allow

They were **licensed** to fish on this part of the river.

licence ⟶ (noun) a permit which allows you to do something

My television **licence** has expired.

stationary ⟶ not moving

The car was **stationary**.   (Think: There is **ar** in c**ar** and station**ar**y!)

stationery ⟶ office paper/envelopes and materials

I ordered some more **stationery** for the office.

(Think: stationery includes paper. There is **er** in pap**er** and station**er**y!)

💡 Tips

Can you find an easy way to remember what a pair of homophones mean?

For example: here or hear ? Hear has **ear** hiding in it!

✔ Skills check

1. Underline the correct homophone for each sentence.

   a. We **heard** / **herd** the firework display in the park.

   b. I wondered **whose** / **who's** car was parked outside my house.

   c. The burglar tried to **steel** / **steal** the television, but it was very heavy.

   d. The porridge was **two** / **to** / **too** hot!

2. Write a sentence for each homophone.

   a. passed _____

     past _____

   b. guessed _____

     guest _____

3. Explain the meaning of each homophone.

   a. aloud _____

     allowed _____

   b. farther _____

     father _____

   c. waste _____

     waist _____

4. Write the other homophone for these words.

   a. great _____

   b. dissent _____

   c. cereal _____

   d. bridal _____

KEY WORD

homophones

Identifying main ideas

Reading

What does identifying main ideas mean?

↻ Recap

When you identify something, you find it in a passage. To find the main ideas, decide what a passage is about overall.

The main ideas are the important things that the author wants the reader to know.

Often there will only be one main idea in a passage but there may be more than one paragraph.

🗒 Revise

Don't worry about each individual idea. Look for something that links them all.

In the passage below there is one main idea.

> The house at the end of our street is very spooky. It is painted black and has tall, thin chimneys. All of the windows are dark and no one ever seems to go in or out.

Each of the sentences is about something different but they are all about the spooky house at the end of the street, so this is the main idea.

💡 Tips

- Try reading the text and then thinking of a **heading** that fits it overall.
- There are sentences on the colour of the house, what it looks like and who goes there. None of these is the main idea.
- Each sentence is about what makes the house **spooky**. So the title would be 'The Spooky House'.

Highlight the words in each sentence that show what the sentence is about. Then find a link between them.

✔ Skills Check

1. Read this passage and identify the main idea.

> People have always been fascinated by the moon. Is it made of cheese? What is on the other side of it? Can human beings live there? Modern science has answered many of these questions and we now know that there is much more to learn about the moon than we already know.

The main idea is:

_____

_____

62

Identifying key details

What does identifying key details involve?

↺ Recap

- Identify means find.
- The main ideas are the important things that the author wants the reader to know.
- The key details are what the author writes about the main ideas.

Revise

Start by identifying the main idea or ideas.

> The city of Hull sits proudly on the north bank of the River Humber. At one time it was the biggest fishing port in the country but now its fishing fleet has disappeared. Nowadays it is a modern city with fast motorway access and direct ferry links to Europe.

← Main idea: how Hull has changed.

Next highlight the points that tell us more about the main idea.

> The city of Hull sits proudly on the north bank of the River Humber. **At one time it was the biggest fishing port in the country** but now **its fishing fleet has disappeared.** Nowadays it is a **modern city** with **fast motorway access** and **direct ferry links to Europe.**

← Each point tells us something different.

Now, use your highlighted points to give three ways that Hull has changed.

1. It is a modern city.
2. It has fast motorway access.
3. It has direct ferry links to Europe.

✔ Skills Check

1. Read the passage below.

> Last summer we had our best holiday ever. We went to Menorca and spent a week splashing about in the pool and on the beach. We laughed all day and never had to worry about going to bed late or getting up early. I made lots of new friends.

a. What is the main idea? _____

b. Give two key details from the text to support this:

1. _____

2. _____

Summarising main ideas

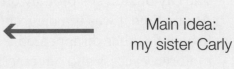

What does summarising ideas mean?

↻ Recap

Summarise means sum up. When you summarise, you say briefly what the passage is about.

A summary might be one word or a complete sentence. You need to find ideas from the whole text.

Revise

You have to read the whole passage before you can summarise.
In the passage below, there are different ideas for each paragraph.

> My sister Carly is very kind. She has a mischievous twinkle in her eyes. She is very popular and makes every day feel like a party.

← Main idea: my sister Carly

> My other sister, Caroline, is very different. She is a very private person who prefers her own company. She has a good sense of humour but rarely uses it outside of the house.

← Main idea: my sister Caroline

There are sentences about two sisters. The link between the two ideas is the difference. Put this together to summarise the main ideas of the paragraphs: the difference between the sisters.

When there is a lot of information in a passage, you might have to write more than one sentence as a summary.

The main idea in the following passage is healthy eating. The reasons that support healthy eating have been highlighted in **blue** and the reasons against it are in **orange**.

Healthy eating

Everybody loves food. Children love fast food. Burgers, chips and nuggets all taste great. There are lots of takeaway shops, meaning that fast food is easy to buy. It isn't always good for you though. Lots of fast food contains large amounts of salt and fat. Salads are really healthy but some people think that they are boring. Healthy eating gives us energy and makes us grow strong. However, if you're busy, a takeaway once in a while won't do you too much harm.

Highlight the key details and then write them in a table.

Reasons against healthy eating	Reasons that support healthy eating
Burgers, chips and nuggets all taste great.	Fast food isn't always good for you.
Fast food is easy to buy.	Fast food contains large amounts of salt and fat.
Some people think that salads are boring.	Salads are really healthy.
A takeaway once in a while won't do you too much harm.	Healthy eating gives us energy and makes us grow strong.

Use the table to help you write a summary. Concentrate on the main points.

Fast food is easy to get and it tastes great. It isn't always good for you because of what it contains. It's important to eat healthy foods like salads but a takeaway occasionally won't harm you too much.

✔ Skills Check

1. **Read the passage below. Fill in the main ideas for each paragraph.**

    a.
    On our street there are three takeaway shops. There is an Indian, a Chinese and an Italian pizza place.

    ← Main idea
    _____

    b.
    We have a different meal every Saturday night. My favourites are lamb rogan josh, chicken chop suey and garlic bread.

    ← Main idea
    _____

2. **Sometimes, the summary is in the form of a heading or subheading.**
    What do you think the best heading for the passage would be? Tick one.

    Favourite food ☐   Saturday night takeaway ☐

    Our street ☐   Fast food ☐

3. **Read the passage below. Highlight the key details, then write a summary.**

    My mother paints pictures. She is really good at landscapes. She's done great pictures of the sea, mountains and lakes. Her portraits aren't as good but she is working on them.

_____

Predicting what might happen

What does predicting mean?

↻ Recap

When you predict you say what you think is likely to happen. Usually you have to give reasons for your ideas. These come from clues that are written in the text.

I see. You have to read the story and say what you think will happen next. This is like being a detective.

📄 Revise

Look at this sentence:

The fire alarm sounded.

To predict what would happen next, you have to look for the clues in the text. In this case the clue has been highlighted. The fire alarm has gone off so what happens next must follow on from that. It has to be realistic, possible and likely. So it is no use predicting that an elephant will arrive, suck up water from a pond and then blow it down its trunk to put the fire out!

The following passage ends with the same sentence. Look at the highlighted clues to help predict what might happen next.

Mia had left the classroom to go to the toilet. On the way back she could smell burning. It was coming from a store room. Mia pushed the door open carefully and saw the flames. She shut the door quickly. Her teacher and her classmates were in the next room. She had to get them out. She punched the red button on the wall. The fire alarm sounded.

What happens next? It would be realistic, possible and likely that the teacher and the pupils would all leave the building. By closing the door, Mia has made sure that fire won't spread quickly, so that should enable the fire brigade to arrive in time to put the fire out.

Read this passage. The last sentence is different.

Mia had left the classroom to go to the toilet. On the way back she could smell burning. It was coming from a store room. Mia pushed the door open carefully and saw the flames. She shut the door quickly. Her teacher and her classmates were in the next room. She had to get them out. She punched the red button on the wall. Nothing happened!

How does changing the ending change your prediction?

You can't keep the same prediction anymore because the clue in the last sentence tells you that something else will have to happen if everyone is to be saved. This gives you a much wider choice of possible predictions.

✔ Skills Check

1. Read this passage. Highlight the important clues.

> Mia hit the button again. Still nothing! She knew she mustn't panic. She ran down the corridor to her classroom and raced inside.
> "The store room is on fire!" she shouted.
> Mrs Milner took control. She told the pupils to leave everything on their desks and to go out of the building as quickly as possible. She made sure everyone had left the classroom and followed them. As she went outside she pressed the red button by the door. The fire alarm sounded.

> Only highlight the points that give clues about what might happen. Use them to make your prediction.

a. What is likely to happen next?

_____

_____

b. Explain why you think this is likely.

_____

_____

2. Read this passage.

> Once the fire was out, the chief fire officer wanted to talk to Mia. She did not know why. He interviewed her in the head teacher's office. When he spoke his tone was very serious.

a. Give two predictions about what the chief fire officer might have wanted to talk to Mia about. You should use information from the whole story in your answer.

1. _____

2. _____

b. Use evidence from the text to explain your answers.

_____

_____

_____

Themes and conventions

What are themes and conventions?

⟳ Recap

- Themes are ideas that go throughout the text.
- Conventions are the things that help you know what type of writing it is.

This table shows you some of the themes and conventions.

Type of writing	Possible themes	Convention of this type of writing
Poetry	love, war	verses, rhyme, rhythm, figurative language
Drama	relationships	speech without inverted commas, stage directions
Fiction	myths and legends, adventure, love, war, good and evil, loss, fear, danger, rich and poor, strong and weak, wisdom and foolishness	heroes and heroines, villains, frightening situations, cliff-hangers, 'good' winning, using stock locations and characters – dark woods and wicked witches
Non-fiction	history, geography, celebrities, sport, gossip, cars and lots of others	textbooks, magazines/newspapers, brochures: headings, subheadings, facts, pictures, columns, bullet points, numbers and dates

You need to be able to identify themes and conventions, and comment on them.

So I need to be able to say how a text is written.

🗒 Revise

In the passage below, the clues to the **theme** have been highlighted.

Only another minute left! Karine's hands fumbled with the fuse. If she cut the wrong wire, it would be the end for all of them. Which wire? Karine didn't know! Thirty seconds. She had to choose one. A 50–50 chance. Red. No green! Fifteen seconds! This was it. Karine would have to cut one now. She held the green wire and hoped!

All of the highlighted words are typical of ones you would find in action stories. The time countdown increases the excitement. These are **conventions**. This is different to the main idea because in this paragraph the main idea would be about defusing the device, which is part of the themes of spy or war novels.

The theme of the passage below is danger. The clues that identify this have been highlighted.

> Stranded high on the ledge, Elliott knew he was in **trouble**. His leg was **broken** and his **radio had been lost** in the fall. Above him, a layer of ice **threatened** to drop down at any moment. He could feel himself **slipping slowly** towards the edge. It was only **a matter of time.**

To comment on the theme, explain what it is.

> **For example:** It follows the tradition that the hero faces immediate death. Everything suggests that the hero cannot survive. The ending makes us think that he will slide over the edge to his doom.

To comment on the conventions, show how they help the reader understand the theme.

> **For example:** The text is an adventure story. It has many of the usual elements including a dangerous location, an injured hero and seemingly inevitable destruction.

✔ Skills Check

> To help identify the theme, highlight the ideas that go throughout the passage.

1. What is the main theme in this passage?

> Dorca the dragon flew across the night sky. Her quest was to find the secret of eternal dragon life. She knew that the knights of Nemore would try to stop her but she had dragon magic on her side!

The main theme is _____.

2. a. Find and copy a phrase that shows that the above passage has this theme.

_____

_____

b. Explain how your phrase or sentence fits this theme.

_____

c. Give two ways that the extract uses the conventions of your chosen theme.

1. _____

2. _____

Explaining and justifying inferences

↻ Recap

- Inferences are assumptions that you make from clues in the text, like how a character is feeling or why something happens. They are the bits the writer doesn't actually tell you but that you can work out for yourself.
- Explain means say what you think.
- Justify means give reasons for what you think, using parts of the text to prove your points.

What does explaining and justifying inferences mean?

OK, so it means read between the lines, work out what is happening and show us why you think that.

Revise

Explaining inferences

Some parts of the text below have been highlighted. These are the clues.

Charlie was really fed up. His day had already been bad and he had a feeling that it was about to get a whole lot worse.

→ The author has told you how Charlie is feeling and why. The only thing to infer is what has made his day bad but there aren't any clues to help you.

Charlie came in from school. He threw his bag into the corner, sighed loudly and kicked the bin.

→ The author has not told you how Charlie is feeling or why. You have to infer that he is unhappy. The clues are in his actions. We still don't know why he is unhappy though.

1. What do the clues in the second part of the text tell us?
Charlie is behaving badly.

2. What do the clues not tell us? Why Charlie is behaving badly.

3. What inference can we make? Charlie is unhappy.

Ask yourself: 'What has happened and how do we know?'

Justifying inferences

You need to give reasons for your thoughts. To do this you need proof. This comes from the clues. In the second part of the text, the three clues that you can use as evidence have been highlighted.

What has happened to make Charlie unhappy?

The author has not told us but we can **infer** from the first sentence that something has happened at school to make Charlie unhappy.

You could try to make inferences about this but it is much more difficult as there isn't any evidence.

Writing answers

Write down an inference that you can make from the passage.

> Charlie is unhappy because of something that has happened at school.

Explain an inference that you can make from the passage.

> When Charlie throws his bag into the corner, sighs loudly and kicks the bin, he is showing he is unhappy. He has just come in from school so it is likely that something has happened there to upset him.

Find and copy two phrases from the text to support your inference.

1. threw his bag
2. sighed loudly

Remember to prove what you think.

✔ Skills Check

1. Read the following passage and answer the questions.

Ella went as slowly as she could into the hall. She wished she had been ill that morning. The maths test was about to take place. The test papers were lying menacingly on the desks. As Ella sat down, she could feel her heartbeat increasing. She wished she had practised more. She took a deep breath and turned the paper over.

a. How do you think Ella is feeling at the start of the passage?

_____

b. Find and copy a phrase that supports your thoughts.

_____

c. Do you think Ella will do well in the test?

_____

d. Use evidence from the text to support your thoughts.

_____

Words in context

What are words in context?

↻ Recap

Words in context means how words are used in the passage.

📄 Revise

Read the following information from a text about eagles.

> There can be few more exciting sights than that of an eagle plummeting towards the earth in pursuit of its prey.

You may not know what 'plummeting' means so read the whole sentence again. The eagle is moving towards the earth. Therefore, 'plummeting' has to be telling us *how* the eagle was moving. It is in 'pursuit of its prey' so it has to be moving quickly.

What does the word 'plummeting' mean in this sentence? Tick one.

descending ☐

diving ☐

sliding ☐

tumbling ☐

In this case, you should tick diving as it fits with 'in pursuit of its prey'.

The other answers all link with 'towards the earth' but they do not give the feeling of speed.

If you don't know what a word means, try to work out what the whole sentence means and see if that gives you any clues.

✔ Skills Check

Read the following passage and answer the question.

> The cliff was uneven. Slowly, bit by bit, hand over hand, I clambered up it.

1. *I clambered up it.*

Which of these words has a similar meaning to 'clambered' in this sentence? Tick one.

walked ☐   climbed ☐

raced ☐   looked ☐

What does exploring words in context mean?

↻ Recap

Explore means to go into the meaning of the words.

Now you have to look at how the words are being used as well.

📄 Revise

To explore, you have to look at a range of possible meanings of a word or phrase.

You may need to read the whole sentence or paragraph again, then work out what the word means.

Read this sentence.

> The price of bread has rocketed in the last five years.

What does 'rocketed' mean in this sentence?

The clue is in the word. What do rockets do? They move quickly; they soar upwards; they go sky high.

To explore the use of 'rocketed', you would need to explain *how* and *why* it is being used in the sentence. **In this context rocketed has been used to show how quickly the price of bread has gone upwards because it reflects the speed of the rise.**

✔ Skills Check

Tips

If you're not sure what a word means in a sentence, read the sentences on each side of it.

Read this passage.

> I do not like rice pudding. There are few foods that I detest more. I avoid it if possible.

1. *There are few foods that I detest more.*
   Which of these words means the same as 'detest' in this sentence? Tick one.

   hate ☐   want ☐

   love ☐   need ☐

Try all of the words and see which one makes most sense when you read the complete sentence.

2. Explain why you have chosen your answer.

_____

_____

Enhancing meaning: figurative language

What is figurative language?

↺ Recap

Figurative language is imagery used by writers to create word pictures that help the readers *see* what is happening and enhances the meaning.

- Examples of this include analogy, metaphors, similes, personification, assonance and alliteration.
- You need to write about the effect of the figurative language.

Revise

Some of the figurative language has been identified in this passage.

> Waves lapped in mournful murmurs against the wreck of the *Free Choice*. The ship lay, a broken-backed corpse, across the reef. Stranded in shallow seas, the vessel groaned like a ghost as each wave hit it.

Figurative language	Type of language	Explain the effect
lapped	personification – because the waves don't really have tongues	Lapped means 'licked'. The description of the action of the waves makes us think about the movement.
mournful murmurs	alliteration – it creates an effect by repeating consonant sounds, in this case the 'm'	Alliteration helps the reader hear the noise.
a broken-backed corpse	metaphor – it compares more strongly, usually using 'is' or 'was'. The metaphor also uses personification to help the reader picture the ship	This metaphor helps us imagine how damaged the ship looks.
groaned like a ghost	simile – it compares by using 'like' or 'as' alliteration	The simile compares the groaning to a ghost, which makes the description more vivid.

It's important to know the name of the figurative language but it's even more important to say what its effect has been.

✔ Skills Check

1. Read the following passage.

> My brother had broken my favourite toy.
> I roared like a monster in anguished anger.
> Tears burned my eyes. My mother, hearing
> my cries, held me like a nurse until I stopped
> sobbing. My father brought the remedy –
> superglue.

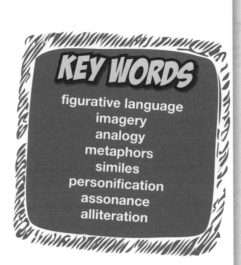

KEY WORDS

figurative language
imagery
analogy
metaphors
similes
personification
assonance
alliteration

a. *I roared like a monster…*
The sentence above contains: Tick **one**.

a metaphor ☐

alliteration ☐

personification ☐

a simile ☐

b. In the table below, highlighted in bold, are examples of figurative language from the passage. In each case, state what type of figurative language is used and explain its effect.

Language used	Type of language and effect
*Tears **burned** my eyes*	
*held me **like a nurse***	
*My father brought the **remedy – superglue**.*	

How writers use language

↻ Recap

How do writers use language?

Writers use language to have an effect on the reader through:
- vocabulary used
- use of different sentence types and links between them
- different types of text (fairy stories, newspapers, magazines, letters).

You have to write about the effect each has on the reader.

Always explain why and how the language that is used affects the reader.

▤ Revise

Words

Different words show different shades of meaning. Some words like '**nice**' or '**good**' are **very vague** and give the reader little idea of what they mean. '**It was a scary film**' could cover anything from **mildly creepy** to **bloodcurdlingly terrifying**. Choosing words carefully is important to ensure that readers know exactly what writers are trying to say.

Sentences

Different forms of sentence create a response in the reader.

- **Everybody loves ice cream.** This is a **statement**. It seems to be a fact but is it? Actually, it's not a fact but it is presented as one so the effect is that the reader believes it is true.
- **Who can argue that Britain is the best country in the world?** This is a **rhetorical question**. It tries to make the reader agree with it by suggesting that no one could argue against it.
- **Finish ahead. Foot flat on the floor! Maximum speed. Go! Go! Go!** These **short sentences** have the effect of making the action seem fast, almost like a series of photographs.

Text

Texts are written for different purposes. You need to be able to identify the purpose and show how the writing fits it. This one is written to inform.

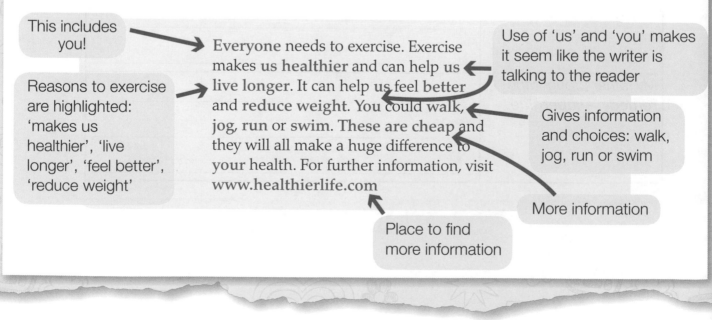

This includes you!

Reasons to exercise are highlighted: 'makes us healthier', 'live longer', 'feel better', 'reduce weight'

Everyone needs to exercise. Exercise makes us healthier and can help us live longer. It can help us feel better and reduce weight. You could walk, jog, run or swim. These are cheap and they will all make a huge difference to your health. For further information, visit www.healthierlife.com

Use of 'us' and 'you' makes it seem like the writer is talking to the reader

Gives information and choices: walk, jog, run or swim

More information

Place to find more information

✔ Skills Check

1. The following questions are about the Exercise extract.

a. Give four reasons why we should exercise.

_____

_____

b. Name two forms of exercise that are recommended.

_____

_____

c. *These are **cheap** and they will all make a **huge** difference to your health.*
What is the effect on the reader of the words in bold?

_____

_____

2. Read this passage.

Run! Run like your life depends on it – because it does.
Run! Don't look back! Run! You'll know when to stop.

Language used	Effect of language
a. *Run!*	What is the effect on the reader of repeating *Run!* _____ _____
b. *because it does*	What is the effect on the reader of this phrase? _____ _____
c. *Don't look back!*	How does this sentence increase the tension or excitement in the passage? _____ _____

💡 Tips

For this question, you have to show which words and writing techniques have been used and what the effect is on the reader.

Features of text

↻ Recap

- Language features – the way the words are used.
- Structural features – the way the text is organised.
- Presentational features – the way the text looks.

📄 Revise

Here are some examples of different features.

Language features	Structural features	Presentational features
• Figurative language • Short/long sentences • Variety/repetition of words • Specific choice of words • Rhetorical questions	• Chapters • Table of contents • Headings and subheadings • Paragraphs or verses	• Pictures and captions • Diagrams • Columns and charts • Text boxes • Fonts and colour

In the following passage, a number of language, structural and presentational features have been identified for you.

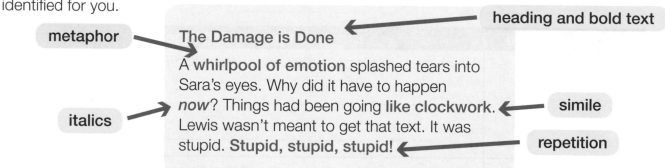

metaphor

italics

heading and bold text

The Damage is Done

A **whirlpool of emotion** splashed tears into Sara's eyes. Why did it have to happen *now*? Things had been going **like clockwork**. Lewis wasn't meant to get that text. It was stupid. **Stupid, stupid, stupid!**

simile

repetition

✔ Skills Check

Why oh why?

Sara stared at her phone. Why had she hit the *send* button?

1. Find and copy examples of language, structural and presentational features from the above text.

Feature	Feature name	Example
Language		
Structural		
Presentational		

Text features contributing to meaning

How do text features contribute to meaning?

↻ Recap

Text features are the language, structural and presentational features of texts.
You need to explain how they help the reader understand the meaning of the text.

Revise

This is the continuation of **The Damage is Done**. Some features are highlighted.

subheading and bold text → **Be careful what you wish for**

short sentence → It was a joke!

She **never meant** to send it. **She never meant** Lewis to get it. **She never** wanted anyone to get hurt. Her phone shook **like an earthquake** in her hand. It was a reply from Lewis.

repetition

simile → like an earthquake

You need to be able to explain how each feature works in the passage as a whole.

Feature	What it does	Explanation
Subheading	Makes it easy to read	Breaks up the text and gives a summary of the main idea of the paragraph
Bold text	Draws attention to important text	Makes it stand out
Short sentence	Increases pace of text	It tells us more about what Sara was doing in a short space of time
Repetition	Reinforces point	Emphasises how little Sara had wanted the events to take place
Simile	Helps the reader imagine the scene	An earthquake is a huge disaster. That is what Sara is expecting when the text comes in

✔ Skills Check

Read both parts of 'The Damage is Done'.

1. How does writing in the third person help the reader?

_____

2. *It was a reply from Lewis.*

How does the writer build up tension in this sentence?

_____

Retrieving and recording information

What does retrieving and recording information mean?

↺ Recap

- Retrieve means find.
- Record means write down.

📄 Revise

Read the following passage. Key pieces of information have been highlighted.

The *Titanic*

The *Titanic* has captured the imagination of the public more than any other ship in history. Perhaps it is because it was **described as 'unsinkable'** by its designer. Perhaps it is because it **sank on its first voyage**. Perhaps it is because there is so much **mystery** surrounding its loss. Whatever the reason, there has been continuous interest in the *Titanic* for **over a hundred years**.

Example questions

What are the reasons people have been interested in the *Titanic*?

Is the same as:

Why have people been interested in the *Titanic*?

Look for the first key words in the question: why, what, who, where, when or how.

Some questions will ask you to join information together. For example, in this case, you might be asked to **draw lines to link the *Titanic* to why people might be interested in it.**

Look for the **other key words in the question**: these tell you what to retrieve from the text. In this question they are: 'interested in the *Titanic*'.

Scan the text above and you'll find three reasons.

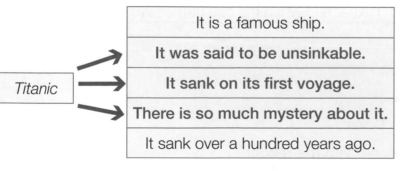

It is a famous ship.
It was said to be unsinkable.
It sank on its first voyage.
There is so much mystery about it.
It sank over a hundred years ago.

Titanic

Tips 💡

Look closely to find the answers.
- **Why** = find a reason
- **Who** = find a name
- **Where** = find a place
- **When** = find a time
- **How** = find an explanation
- **What** can be any of the above.

✔ Skills Check

1. Read 'The *Titanic*' again.

a. Who is interested in the *Titanic*?

_____

b. How long is it since the *Titanic* sank?

_____

c. Why would people be surprised that it sank?

_____

d. Interest in the *Titanic* has been: Tick **one**.

increasing. ☐

reducing. ☐

continuous. ☐

overwhelming. ☐

Remember to look for the key words. They tell you what to retrieve.

2. Read the continuation of 'The *Titanic*'.

Nowadays the *Titanic* lies at the bottom of the Atlantic Ocean. It is still recognisable as the wonderful ship it once was, even though it is encrusted with barnacles and sea life. Instead of the rich and the famous, it is now home to a whole host of different sea creatures. There are memorials to the *Titanic* in Belfast, Liverpool, Southampton, Washington DC and New York. Although there is still huge interest in it, it will probably never be brought to the surface.

Draw lines to link the *Titanic* with information about it nowadays.

It is at the bottom of the Pacific Ocean.
It looks just like it did before it sank.
Sea creatures now live in it.
There are memorials in five cities.
It will be raised soon.

Titanic

Making comparisons

What does making comparisons mean?

Revise

Read the following passage.

My favourite birds

My hobby is bird watching, or ornithology, to give it its proper name. Why have two names? Well, it's a bit like the birds themselves. They all have common names but they also all have proper names. Did you know that sparrows are also called Passeridae? No? Neither did I until I started watching them.

I don't really like little birds. My favourites are the hunting birds. I love owls. They are so graceful. They fly in silence, seemingly without effort. Some people don't like them at all. They see them as cruel hunters. They prefer birds that don't even fly, like penguins, but they hunt too. People like the awkward way they walk. What's the point in a bird that can't fly? It's like a fish that's scared of water.

Give one reason why people might like owls and one why they might not.

Like owls: They are graceful or they fly in silence, seemingly without effort.

Dislike owls: They are seen as cruel hunters.

Read the continuation of the passage.

Owls glide through the air in pursuit of their prey. Penguins can't fly but they do the same underwater. An owl in flight is a graceful sight. Penguins are equally graceful in the water. Owls hop while penguins walk. Neither bird is particularly comfortable on the ground but of the two, penguins are more suited to being on land. Owls can be found in the wild all over the world but penguins only live in the southern hemisphere.

To compare, you have to show the similarities and the differences.

Comparison	Owls	Penguins
Similarities – movement	Graceful in flight	Graceful in water
Differences – movement	Hop	Walk
Differences – where they live	All over the world	In the southern hemisphere

✔ Skills check

1. Read the continuation of the 'My favourite birds' passage again.

  a. Give one thing that is different between owls and penguins.

  _____

  b. Give one thing that is similar between owls and penguins.

  _____

2. Read the following passage.

Some animals are more popular than others. For instance, cats are almost universally liked while snakes are hated the world over. I am perfectly happy to have my cat slide onto my knee and settle down to watch television with me. I can't say the same of a snake. Why? Cats are much more familiar to us so their danger seems less. Cats do not hunt large prey, like us. Snakes? Well, what do we know? They hiss and spit but so do cats when they are annoyed. Snakes hunt small animals. So do cats.

Don't get yourself tied up in knots. To compare just show similarities and differences.

  a. Compare the author's attitude to cats and snakes.

  _____

  _____

  _____

  b. What is similar between cats and snakes?

  _____

  _____

  c. What differences are there between cats and snakes?

  _____

  _____

Find the key words in the question and look for them in the text.

Fact and opinion

↻ Recap

What is fact and opinion?

- A **fact** is true and can be proved.
- An **opinion** is what someone thinks or believes.

You need to be able to tell the difference between facts and opinions.

To tell if something is a fact, ask: 'Can it be proved?'

📄 Revise

In the passage below, there is one **fact** and one **opinion**.

> Jessica Ennis-Hill won a gold medal in the heptathlon at the London Olympics in 2012. She is the most talented heptathlete Britain will ever have.

- Jessica Ennis-Hill did win the Olympic gold medal. **Can this be proved? Yes.** There is video evidence to prove it. She is the most talented...will ever have. **Can this be proved? No.** Nobody knows what will happen in the future.

- The text makes it seems as if Jessica is the most talented heptathelete. How? It starts with a fact that proves that she is a top-class athlete and therefore implies she is the most talented. We might believe the second sentence is a fact because we know that the first one is but there is no way we can predict the future and what new heptathletes Britain will have in the future.

Read the following passage.

> The tallest mountain in Wales is Mount Snowdon. It is known in Welsh as Yr Wyddfa.

How many **facts** are in the passage? **Two.**
Both sentences contain **facts** that can be proved.

Tips

> At 1085 metres high, Yr Wyddfa is the highest mountain in Wales. You can walk to the top or, for the less energetic, there is the Snowdon Mountain Railway.

Watch out for **'foggy phrases'**. They're hard to see through and it's easy to get lost in them! 'Everybody knows' and 'There can be no doubt' are foggy phrases. They make things seem like **facts** when really they are **opinions**.

✔ Skills Check

Read the following passage.

> I think that the Mona Lisa is a strange picture. Painted by Leonardo da Vinci and also called La Gioconda, it is kept in the Louvre in Paris. It is only 77cm by 53cm and is hung in a dark room to avoid the light damaging it. When I went, the room was packed with people trying to see the picture. It was not awe-inspiring. The statue of Venus de Milo is much more impressive. It's not worth queuing to see the Mona Lisa. You'd be better off spending your time in the Egyptian section. The sphinx in there is really impressive.

1. **Put a tick in the correct box to show whether each of the following statements are fact or opinion.**

	Fact	Opinion
The Mona Lisa is 77cm by 53cm.		
The Mona Lisa is a strange picture.		
The Mona Lisa is not awe-inspiring.		
The Mona Lisa is in a dark room.		

> Sentences that include 'I think' or 'I believe' are opinions. Don't be fooled. Remember, facts can be proved.

2. **Find and copy three facts from the passage that are not included in the table above.**

   1. _____

   2. _____

   3. _____

3. **Find and copy three opinions that are not included in the table above.**

   1. _____

   2. _____

   3. _____

Glossary

active voice is when the subject does the action. The school arranged a visit.

adjectives are sometimes called 'describing words' because they pick out features of nouns such as size or colour. They can be used before or after a noun, to give more detail. The red bus.

adverbs can describe the manner, time, place or cause of something. They tell you more information about the event or action.

adverbials are words or phrases that give us more information about an event or action. They tell you how, when, where or why something happened.

alliteration is the repetition of a consonant sound or letter in several words: beautiful black butterfly.

analogy is a comparison in which an idea is compared to something that is quite different. It compares the idea to something that is familiar to the reader. There are plenty more fish in the sea.

antonyms are words with opposite meanings. Hot – cold; light – dark.

apostrophes:
- show the place of missing letters (**contraction**)
- show who or what something belongs to (**possession**).

assonance is the repetition of a vowel sound in several words: aggressive angry alligator.

auxiliary verbs are be, have, do and the **modal verbs**.

B

brackets show parenthesis. They are placed around extra information in a sentence. Alex (who had got up late) ran all the way to school.

C

clauses are groups of words that must contain a subject and a verb. Clauses can sometimes be complete sentences.
- **main clause:** contains a subject and verb and makes sense on its own.
- **subordinate clause:** needs the rest of the sentence to make sense. A subordinate clause includes a conjunction to link it to the main clause.
- **relative clause:** is a type of subordinate clause that changes a noun. It uses relative pronouns such as who, which or that to refer back to that noun.

colons are used to introduce a list, quotations and for separating two equal clauses.

command tells someone to do something and ends with an exclamation mark or a full stop.

commas have different uses including:
- to separate items in a list
- to separate a fronted adverbial from the rest of the sentence
- to clarify meaning
- to show parenthesis.

common noun (boy, man) names something in general.

conjunctions link two words, phrases or clauses together. There are two main types of conjunction:
- **co-ordinating conjunctions** (and, but) link two equal clauses together.
- **subordinating conjunctions** (when, because) link a subordinate clause to a main clause.

consonants are most of the letters of the alphabet except the vowel letters a, e, i, o, u

contraction a shortened word where an apostrophe shows the place of missing letters.

co-ordinating conjunctions (and, but) link two equal clauses together.

D

dashes in pairs show parenthesis. A single dash can also be used instead of a colon.

determiners go before a noun (or noun phrase) and show which noun you are talking about.

direct speech is what is actually spoken by someone. The actual words spoken will be enclosed in **inverted commas**: "Please can I have a drink?"

E

ellipsis is the omission of a word or phrase which is expected and predictable. Where are you going? (To) the shops. Ellipsis = to.

exclamation expresses excitement, emotion or surprise and ends with an exclamation mark.

F

figurative language uses words and ideas to create a mental image. Imagery, metaphors, similes and personification are all types of figurative language.

fronted adverbials are at the start of a sentence. They are usually followed by a comma.

future time is shown in a number of different ways. These all involve the use of a present tense verb. We will go to the park. We are going home tomorrow.

H

homophones are words that sound the same but are spelled differently and mean different things.

hyphens are used to join words together or to clarify meaning. A man-eating shark.

I

imagery uses words that create a picture of ideas in our minds.

inverted commas (also known as speech marks) are punctuation that enclose direct speech: "Please can I have a drink?"

M

main clause: contains a subject and verb and makes sense on its own

metaphors describe something as being something else, even though it is <u>not</u> actually that. The moon was a ghostly galleon.

modal verbs tell us how likely it is that something will happen.

N

nouns are sometimes called 'naming words' because they name people, places and things.
- **proper noun** (Ivan, Wednesday) names something specifically and starts with a capital letter.
- **common noun** (boy, man) names something in general.

noun phrases are phrases with nouns as their main word and may contain adjectives or prepositions: enormous grey elephant/in the garden.

O

object is normally a noun, pronoun or noun phrase that shows what the verb is acting upon.

P

parenthesis is a word, clause or phrase inserted into a sentence to add more detail.

passive voice is when the subject has the action performed on it. The sentence It was eaten by our dog is the passive of Our dog ate it.

past tense describes past events. Most verbs take the suffix ed to form their past tense.

perfect form of a verb usually talks about a past event and uses the verb have + another verb.
- **past perfect**: He had gone to lunch.
- **present perfect**: He has gone to lunch.

personal pronouns replace people or things.

personification is when human qualities are given to an animal, object or thing.

phrase is a group of words that are grammatically connected so that they stay together, and that expand a single word. Phrases do not contain a subject or a verb.

plural means 'more than one'.

possession a word that shows who or what something belongs to using an apostrophe.

possessive pronouns are used to show who something belongs to.

prefix is is a set of letters added to the beginning of a word in order to turn it into another word.

prepositions link nouns (or pronouns or noun phrases) to other words in the sentence. Prepositions usually tell you about place, direction or time.

present tense describes actions that are happening now.

progressive or 'continuous' form of a verb describes events in progress. We are singing.

pronouns are short words used to replace nouns (or noun phrases) so that the noun does not need to be repeated.
- **personal pronouns** replace people or things.
- **possessive pronouns** are used to show who something belongs to.
- **relative pronouns** introduce a relative clause and are used to start a description about a noun.

proper noun (Ivan, Wednesday) names something specifically and starts with a capital letter.

Q

question asks a question and ends with a question mark.

R

relative clause is a type of subordinate clause that changes a noun. It uses relative pronouns such as who, which or that to refer back to that noun.

relative pronouns introduce a relative clause and are used to start a description about a noun.

root word is a word to which new words can be made by adding prefixes and suffixes: happy – unhappy – happiness.

S

semi-colons can be used to separate longer items in a list and to separate two unequal clauses.

sentence is a group of words which have a subject and verb and make sense. There are different types of sentence:

- **statement** is a fact which ends with a full stop.
- **question** asks a question and ends with a question mark.
- **command** tells someone to do something and ends with an exclamation mark or a full stop.
- **exclamation** expresses excitement, emotion or surprise and ends with an exclamation mark.

similes use words such as 'like' or 'as' to make a direct comparison.

singular means 'only one'.

statement is a fact which ends with a full stop.

subject of a verb is normally the noun, noun phrase or pronoun that names the 'do-er' or 'be-er'.

subjunctive is used in formal language. I wish I were...

subordinate clause needs the rest of the sentence to make sense. A subordinate clause includes a conjunction to link it to the main clause.

subordinating conjunctions (when, because) link a subordinate clause to a main clause.

suffix is a word ending or a set of letters added to the end of a word to turn it into another word.

syllable sounds like a beat in a word. Longer words have more than one syllable.

synonyms have the same or a similar meaning.

T

tense is **present** or **past** tense and normally shows differences of time.

V

verbs are doing or being words. They describe what is happening in a sentence. Verbs come in different tenses.

vowel sounds are made with the letters a, e, i, o, u. Y can also represent a vowel sound.

W

word families are groups of words that are linked to each other by letter pattern or meaning.

Word lists These are the words you need to learn to spell.

Years 3–4

accident	certain	famous	island	peculiar	sentence
accidentally	circle	favourite	knowledge	perhaps	separate
actual	complete	February	learn	popular	special
actually	consider	forward/	length	position	straight
address	continue	forwards	library	possess	strange
answer	decide	fruit	material	possession	strength
appear	describe	grammar	medicine	possible	suppose
arrive	different	group	mention	potatoes	surprise
believe	difficult	guard	minute	pressure	therefore
bicycle	disappear	guide	natural	probably	though/
breath	early	heard	naughty	promise	although
breathe	earth	heart	notice	purpose	thought
build	eight/eighth	height	occasion	quarter	through
busy/business	enough	history	occasionally	question	various
calendar	exercise	imagine	often	recent	weight
caught	experience	increase	opposite	regular	woman/
centre	experiment	important	ordinary	reign	women
century	extreme	interest	particular	remember	

Years 5–6

accommodate	communicate	equip	immediately	physical	sincerely
accompany	community	equipped	individual	prejudice	soldier
according	competition	equipment	interfere	privilege	stomach
achieve	conscience	especially	interrupt	profession	sufficient
aggressive	conscious	exaggerate	language	programme	suggest
amateur	controversy	excellent	leisure	pronunciation	symbol
ancient	convenience	existence	lightning	queue	system
apparent	correspond	explanation	marvellous	recognise	temperature
appreciate	criticise	familiar	mischievous	recommend	thorough
attached	curiosity	foreign	muscle	relevant	twelfth
available	definite	forty	necessary	restaurant	variety
average	desperate	frequently	neighbour	rhyme	vegetable
awkward	determined	government	nuisance	rhythm	vehicle
bargain	develop	guarantee	occupy	sacrifice	yacht
bruise	dictionary	harass	occur	secretary	
category	disastrous	hindrance	opportunity	shoulder	
cemetery	embarrass	identity	parliament	signature	
committee	environment	immediate	persuade	sincere	

Answers: Year 6

GRAMMATICAL WORDS

Page 6

1 **a.** The <u>mischievous</u> toddler hid in the <u>large</u> cupboard.
   b. It was a <u>disastrous</u> start to their <u>annual</u> holiday.

2 Accept any appropriate substitution of *nice*, for example
   a. Josh wrote a **fantastic** story.
   b. Aliah enjoyed the **exciting** pantomime.

3 Accept appropriate adjectives, for example
   a. sleepy, snowy
   b. massive, vicious

Page 7

1

Word	Common noun	Proper noun
summer	✓	
Turkey		✓
pleasure	✓	

Page 8

1

Present tense	Past tense	Present progressive	Past progressive
she brings	she **brought**	**she is bringing**	**she was bringing**
they catch	they caught	**they are catching**	**they were catching**
it grows	**it grew**	it is **growing**	**it was growing**
we build	we built	**we are building**	**we were building**

2 They **were working** hard when the fire alarm stopped them.

Page 9

1 **a.** He **has gone** out to play.
   b. They **have developed** a method for baking perfect bread.

2 I **had enjoyed** the film until the end spoilt it.

Page 10

1 I **saw/see** a bird in the garden.

2 has accompanied

Page 11

1 We <u>could</u> stay in on Saturday night but we <u>might</u> go to the cinema instead.

2 George **must/should/ought to** improve his backhand if he wants to win the tennis match.

3 Emma will buy some jeans on Saturday. ✓

Page 12

1 **a.** He (gently) stroked the frightened kitten.
   b. They ran (desperately) to catch the train.

2 Accept any appropriate adverb, for example
   a. She **quickly** opened the enormous parcel.
   b. We **desperately** searched the gloomy forest.

Page 13

1

Sentence	Adverb of time	Adverb of place	Adverb of manner
Rarely has the show been so successful.	✓		
She practised **hard** for the piano test.			✓
They didn't know the treasure was **nearby**.		✓	

Page 14

1 Answers may vary, For example:
   a. It is **definitely** six miles to town.
   b. I can **possibly** come to see you later.
   c. Maybe we can have tea together?

2 Accept any appropriate explanation, for example
   Clearly suggests they expect to win.
   Possibly suggests some doubt about whether they will win.

Page 15

1 In the garden, the puppies played happily.

2 Accept any appropriate fronted adverbial, for example
   After rushing, they arrived at the party early.

Page 16

1

Group of words	Clause	Not a
they came home	✓	
because they		✓
it was a wonderful beach holiday	✓	

2 **a.** Despite the long delay, <u>they arrived on time</u>.
   b. <u>They studied hard</u> for their test.

Page 17

1 Accept any appropriate main clause, for example
   They took the dog for a walk in the evening.
   I love pizza, although I can't make one.

2 Accept any subordinate clause which makes sense, for example
   a. I watched television until **it was bedtime**.
   b. We haven't got much bread though **there is enough for a sandwich**.

Page 18

1 **a.** My new bike was light **so** I was able to go very fast.
   b. I like curry **but** I don't like it very spicy.
   c. I wasn't able to score a goal **nor** was I able to help my team score.

2 **a.** I wanted a new tablet **but** they were very expensive.
   b. The house was very cold **but** the central heating was on.

Page 19

1 **a.** I can't go swimming **unless** you give me a lift.
   b. I will go out with you **if/since/as** you are free.

2 Accept any appropriate subordinate clause, for example
   a. More people came in after **the play started**.
   b. Even though you are my elder sister **you are shorter than me**.

Page 20

1 Accept any appropriate relative clause, for example
   a. The hotel, **which we liked**, was next to the beach.
   b. August, **when it is school holidays**, is very busy.

Sentence	Main Clause	Subordinate clause	Relative clause
The rain, **which fell heavily**, made us cancel the trip.			✓
We called at Tomas's house **after we had seen Josh**.		✓	
Unless you are able to pay tomorrow, **the trip will be full.**	✓		

90

1 **a.** Alicia enjoyed the party but **she** didn't like the food.
   b. George and Oscar went sledging which **they** found enthralling.

2 **a.** I have never used my <u>fountain pen</u> as **it** is too messy!
   b. <u>John and I</u> both devoured **our** food.

1 **a.** The hawk circled **around** its prey.
   b. He took the milk **out of** the fridge.

2 Accept any sentences which use beneath and across appropriately, for example
   He found the mushrooms **beneath** the tree.
   She kicked the football **across** the park.

1 **a.** I washed **my** face with **some** soap.
   b. We climbed up **the** stairs and reached **our** bedrooms.

2 (Every) child must pay (some) money for (the) school trip.

1 **a.** My (mum) drove the car.
   b. Our (cat) ate its food.

2 **a.** Dad is making (tea).
   b. The dog chased the (cat).

1

Sentence	Active	Passive
The winning shot was made by Alisha.		✓
The team won the league.	✓	
Small mammals are hunted by eagles.		✓
Many people have climbed Mount Everest.	✓	

2 A wonderful meal was made by the chef.

1 **a.** It is important that you **be** on time for the show.
   b. If I **were** you, I would take the risk.

2 **a.** If I <u>were</u> to give you £25, what would you do with it?
   b. The teacher asked that her students <u>be</u> quieter.

PUNCTUATION

1 It is a sunny day. → statements
   Is it sunny? → questions
   What time does it start? → questions
   We can start it soon. → statements

2 Accept any question starting with the word 'When', for example
   When can we go to the cinema?

Sentence	Statement	Question	Exclamation	Command
Do you want a new bicycle		✓		
Racing bikes are very aerodynamic	✓			
What an amazing bicycle			✓	
Ride this bike				✓

Accept any appropriate exclamation, starting with 'How', for example **How fantastic of you to come!**

1 **a.** You won't be late, <u>will you</u>?
   b. We're going to the cinema, <u>aren't we</u>?

2 **a.** You'd like pizza for tea, **wouldn't you**?
   b. This is the right answer, **isn't it**?

1 **a.** I wonder if (it'll) be sunny later.
   b. I (should've) sent a birthday card to my gran.

2 **a.** hadn't
   b. could've
   c. we'd

1 **a.** The girls' bags
   b. The boy's crayons

2 The trains' arrivals were all delayed by the weather.

1 **a.** We had Jack, Amir, Rashid and Josef on our team.
   b. The children enjoyed their picnic of sausage rolls, egg sandwiches, apples, crisps and juice.

2 Europe is made up of many countries including Britain, France, Spain, Germany and Italy. ✓

1 **a.** My favourite city is Paris, which is the capital of France.
   b. Paris, which is my favourite city, is the capital of France.

1 **a.** My mum loves cooking, my dad and me.
   b. Nate invited two boys, John and Eddy.
   c. My uncle, a singer and a dancer, often appeared on television.
   d. Has the cat eaten, Callum?

1 **a.** Grim and sinister, the graveyard lay before me.
   b. After lunch, we had geography and art.
   c. Patiently, I waited my turn.
   d. While the lead singer sang loudly, the guitarist played the backing tune.
   e. Silently and softly, the snow fell outside.
   f. Running to catch the bus, I tripped and fell.

2 Accept any appropriate fronted adverbial, for example
   Despite forgetting to buy the burgers, it was a wonderful barbeque.

1 **a.** "We can sit over there," said Demi.
   b. Sherri said, **"This punctuation stuff is easy."**

2 **a.** Donny said, "I like eating cream cakes."
   b. "They're not good for you," replied Shirley. or "They're not good for you!" replied Shirley.

3 **a.** My sister said, "On Sunday we are going to Nan's for tea."
   b. The driver said, "This bus is going to town."

1 **a.** You will need to bring with you: your passport, plane tickets, money, sun cream and sunglasses.
   b. We now know some countries that border the Mediterranean Sea: Egypt, France, Spain and Italy.
   c. Warm waters can be found in: the Mediterranean Sea, the Caribbean Sea and the Indian Ocean.
   d. In *Julius Caesar*, Shakespeare wrote: "There is a tide in the affairs of men, which taken at the flood, leads on to fortune."
   e. Phoebe often wears sunglasses: the bright light hurts her eyes.

2 May has thirty days; so does June.

3 I need to go to: the supermarket for some dog food; the heel bar where my shoes have been mended; and the library to get some books for my history project.

4 Water boils at 100 degrees Celsius at sea level; it freezes at 0 degrees.

Page 41

1 **a.** The three men (they looked like spies to me) talked quietly in the corner of the cafe.
b. Denny, my older brother, is joining the army.
c. Suki – a long-haired Alsatian – won first prize at the dog show.
d. I had to keep very still while the doctor, who was very gentle, took my stitches out. (Accept dashes or brackets in place of the commas.)
e. A massive hurricane – the strongest wind ever – will hit this country, probably on Tuesday next week. *or* A massive hurricane, the strongest wind ever, will hit this country – probably on Tuesday next week.

Page 42

1 My mother-in-law is coming for Sunday lunch.

2 My uncle, a retired surgeon, showed me some of his little-used instruments.

3 re-sign

Page 43

1 **a.** My son was born <u>at the start of this century,</u> in 2001. or My son was born at the start of this century, <u>in 2001.</u>
b. I went because I wanted to <u>go</u>.
c. My sister likes salad but I don't <u>like salad</u>.

2 **a.** "**No** we don't."
b. "**Yes** I have.
c. "My dad **does**."

Page 44

1 **law. // Outside**. Reason: change of place.

Page 45

1 **a.** 'The way we speak' or similar. Accept answers that summarise the entire passage.
b. 'My cousins' speech' or similar. Accept answers that refer to differences in pronunciation.

VOCABULARY

Page 46

1 complex ✓ arduous ✓ intricate ✓

2
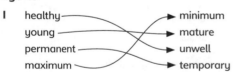
ancient → genuine
curious → antique
familiar → inquisitive
sincere → known

Page 47

1
healthy → minimum
young → mature
permanent → unwell
maximum → temporary

2 Accept any appropriate antonyms, for example
a. I **destroyed** a massive tower.
b. The successful man was very **arrogant**.
c. The **sensible** child had no packed lunch.

Page 48

1 **a.** **im**mature
b. **ir**relevant
c. **in**accessible
d. **il**legible

2 **a.** Emily had several (incorrect) answers.
b. They waited (impatiently) to be chosen for the team.
c. An (irregular) hexagon has six unequal sides.

Page 49

1
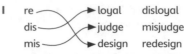
re — loyal   disloyal
dis — judge   misjudge
mis — design   redesign

2 replace, miscalculate, distasteful

Page 50

1 **a.** malic**ious**
b. infec**tious**
c. vigor**ous**
d. mountain**ous**

2 **a.** (religious)
b. (conscientious)

Page 51

1

Start of word	ant or ent?	ance or ence?	ancy or ency?
dec	**decent**		**decency**
confid	**confident**	**confidence**	
toler	**tolerant**	**tolerance**	**tolerancy**
obedi	**obedient**	**obedience**	

2 **a.** The (non-existence) of dodos in Mauritius has long been a cause for regret.
b. Your help is more of a (hindrance).
c. Please complete the (relevant) application form.

Page 53

1 **a.** Any two from: critical, criticise, critisim
b. Any two from: dependent, dependant, dependable, depending, depended
c. Any two from: achievable, achieving, achieved, achievement

2

Word	Root word	Suffix	Prefix
impatience	**patient**	**ence**	**im**
unfriendly	**friend**	**ly**	**un**
disappointment	**appoint**	**ment**	**dis**

3 **a.** disembark
b. indecent
c. maternal

4 **a.** enchant
b. enthral
c. apply

SPELLING

Page 54

1 **a.** They **sought** a way out of the forest, but it was hard to find.
b. I **brought** some toys with me.
c. They installed a new **wrought** iron gate.
d. We **bought** some cakes to have with our sandwiches.

2
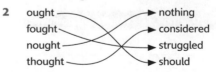
ought → nothing
fought → considered
nought → struggled
thought → should

Page 55

1 **a.** They **roughly** worked out how to make the model.
b. The doors were made of **toughened** glass.
c. We bought some **doughnuts** to eat at the fairground.

2

Definition	Word
area	**borough**
branch	**bough**
cultivate	**plough**
sufficient	**enough**
animal food container	**trough**

Page 56

1 **a.** They went over the bridge to the I<u>s</u>le of Anglesey.
b. Look at the third colum<u>n</u>.
c. We are inde<u>b</u>ted to you, thanks to all your efforts.
d. Caitlin saw a Mis<u>t</u>le Thrush in the garden.

2 **a.** doubt
b. isle
c. condemn
d. bristle

Page 57

1 **a.** I went twice to call on Ahmed.
b. There was a very fierce dog behind the gate.
c. It was bliss sitting in the hot sun.
d. Our teacher suggested that we read books by Michael Morpurgo.

2 **a.** practice
b. piece

Page 58

1

Word	1 pair	2 pairs
guarantee	✓	
accidentally		✓
pressurised	✓	
immediate	✓	

2 **a.** appreciate
b. opportunity
c. committee
d. interrupt

Page 59

1 **a.** immediately: double **m**; **iat**; is there an end **e** before **y**?
b. necessary: 1 **c** but 2 **s**; soft **s** made with **c**.

2 **a.** government
b. marvellous
c. recognise

Page 61

1 **a.** We <u>heard</u> the firework display in the park.
b. I wondered <u>whose</u> car was parked outside my house.
c. The burglar tried to <u>steal</u> the television, but it was very heavy.
d. The porridge was <u>too</u> hot!

2 Accept any appropriate sentence using each homophone, for example
a. My sister **passed** her driving test.
You need to meet me at half **past** three.
b. We **guessed** that you wouldn't arrive until late.
I helped mum prepare the **guest** bedroom.

a. aloud: to say something out loud
allowed: you need permission
b. farther: beyond; at a distance
father: dad
c. waste: rubbish/not making the best of
waist: middle of your body, between chest and hips

a. grate
b. descent
c. serial
d. bridle

READING

Page 62

1 what we know about the moon

Page 63

1 **a.** Last year's holiday in Menorca.
b. Any two forms of: 1. We spent a week in the pool and on the beach.
2. We never had to worry about going to bed late or getting up early.
3. Lots of new friends.

Page 65

1 **a.** Types of takeaway shops
b. Favourite takeaway meals

2 Saturday night takeaway ✓

3 Summary: My mother paints great landscapes but she is not as good at painting portraits.

Page 67

1 Mia hit the button again. Still nothing! She knew she mustn't panic. She ran down the corridor to her classroom and raced inside.
"The store room is on fire!" she shouted.
Mrs Milner took control. She told the pupils to leave everything on their desks and to go out of the building as quickly as possible. She made sure everyone had left the classroom and followed them. As she went outside she pressed the red button by the door. The fire alarm sounded.
a. The pupils are all safe outside the building. The fire brigade comes and puts out the fire.
b. These are the next logical steps from the clues in the passage.

2 **a.** He might congratulate her on saving all of the pupils and the teacher, or he might want to question her about how the fire started or how she found it.
b. Congratulate: She has saved the school. She did the correct things. She didn't panic when the fire alarm didn't work. Question: His tone was serious. She was 'interviewed'. It took place in the head teacher's office. She was alone when she found the fire. The fire alarm didn't work at first.

Page 69

1 Myth

2 **a.** Possible answers: Dorca the dragon, quest, secret of eternal dragon life, knights of Nemore, dragon magic
b. Each phrase has stereotypical elements of myths.
c. Any two from: flying dragons, knights, quests and magic.

Page 71

1 **a.** Scared, worried, apprehensive or similar.
b. 'Ella went as slowly as she could into the hall' or 'She wished she had been ill that morning'.
c. No.
d. 'She wished she had practised more' shows she has not done enough work to do well. 'The test papers were lying menacingly on the desks' suggests that she feels threatened by them.

Page 72

1 climbed

Page 73

1 hate

2 The first sentence says the writer does not like rice pudding. The last one says the writer avoids it. Hate is the only word that would fit with these two sentences.

Page 75

1 **a.** a simile

b.

Language used	Type of language and effect
Tears **burned** my eyes	**This is a metaphor showing the heat of the tears.**
Held me **like a nurse**	**The simile shows how the mother cared for the writer until he was well again.**
My father brought the **remedy – superglue.**	**This is a metaphor. The superglue acts like a medicine to cure everything.**

Page 77

1 **a.** Exercise can make us healthier; help us live longer; help us feel better; help us to reduce weight.

b. Two from: walk, jog, run or swim.

c. Cheap – indicates that exercise need not be expensive. Huge – indicates amount of difference. Both words are meant to persuade the reader to exercise.

2 **a.** 'Run!' makes the reader feel as if they are being given the instruction. The repetition emphasises how important it is to run. It makes the passage scary because you do not know why you are running.

b. It emphasises the need to run because your life is in danger if you don't.

c. It increases the tension because it warns you but it doesn't tell you what is there. It increases the excitement because it makes you feel that whatever is chasing you is right behind you. It makes it seem like whatever is there is too scary to look at.

Page 78

1

Feature	Feature name	Example
Language	**rhetorical question**	**Why had she hit the send button?**
Structural	**heading**	**Why oh why?**
Presentational	**italics**	**send**

Page 79

1 It enables readers to see and hear everything as if they were there. They are able to know what Sara is thinking.

2 It leaves the passage on a cliffhanger. The readers do not know what Lewis's text will say but they can guess from what has gone before.

Page 81

1 **a.** The public

b. Over one hundred years

c. It was described as unsinkable

d. continuous

2

Titanic	→	Sea creatures now live in it.
	→	There are memorials in five cities.

Page 83

1 **a.** One from: Owls hop and penguins walk. Penguins can swim, owls can't. Owls can fly, penguins can't.

b. The way they move (graceful) or where they live (in the wild). Accept specific details.

2 **a.** The author would let a cat slide onto his/her knee but would not do the same with a snake.

b. Cats and snakes both hiss and spit. They both hunt small animals.

c. Cats are almost universally liked while snakes are hated the world over.

Page 85

1

	Fact	Opinion
The Mona Lisa is 77cm by 53cm.	✓	
The Mona Lisa is a strange picture.		✓
The Mona Lisa is not awe-inspiring.		✓
The Mona Lisa is in a dark room.	✓	

2 The Mona Lisa was painted by Leonardo da Vinci. It is also called La Gioconda. It is in the Louvre.

3 Any three from: The statue of Venus de Milo is much more impressive. It's not worth queuing to see the Mona Lisa. You'd be better off spending your time in the Egyptian section. The sphinx in there is really impressive.

Revision planner

Grammatical words

Revised	Achieved		
☐	☐	Adjectives	6
☐	☐	Nouns and noun phrases	7
☐	☐	Verbs: present and past tense	8
☐	☐	Verbs: present perfect and past perfect tense	9
☐	☐	Verbs: tense consistency and Standard English	10
☐	☐	Modal verbs	11
☐	☐	Adverbs	12
☐	☐	Adverbs and adverbials of time, place and manner	13
☐	☐	Adverbs of possibility	14
☐	☐	Fronted adverbials	15
☐	☐	Clauses	16
☐	☐	Main and subordinate clauses	17
☐	☐	Co-ordinating conjunctions	18
☐	☐	Subordinating conjunctions	19
☐	☐	Relative clauses	20
☐	☐	Personal and possessive pronouns	21
☐	☐	Prepositions	22
☐	☐	Determiners	23
☐	☐	Subjects and objects	24
☐	☐	Active and passive verbs	25
☐	☐	Subjunctive	26

Punctuation

Revised	Achieved		
☐	☐	Sentence types: statements and questions	27
☐	☐	Sentence types: exclamations and commands	28
☐	☐	Question tags	29
☐	☐	Apostrophes: contraction	30
☐	☐	Apostrophes: possession	31
☐	☐	Commas in lists	32
☐	☐	Commas to separate clauses	33
☐	☐	Commas to clarify meaning	34
☐	☐	Commas after fronted adverbials	35
☐	☐	Inverted commas	36
☐	☐	Colons and semi-colons	38
☐	☐	Parenthesis	40
☐	☐	Hyphens	42
☐	☐	Ellipsis	43
☐	☐	Paragraphs	44
☐	☐	Headings and subheadings	45

Vocabulary

Spelling

Reading